BASIL
HENRIQUES
A Portrait

Plate 1 Basil, aged sixty-eight, on the occasion of a BBC talk, 1958

BASIL
HENRIQUES
A Portrait

Based on his diaries, letters and
speeches as collated by his widow,
Rose Henriques

L. L. Loewe

Foreword by

The Rt Hon. The Viscount Amory,
KG, PC, GCMG, TD, DL

London, Henley and Boston
Routledge & Kegan Paul

First published in 1976
by Routledge & Kegan Paul Ltd
39 Store Street,
London WC1E 7DD,
Broadway House,
Newtown Road,
Henley-on-Thames,
Oxon RG9 1EN and
9 Park Street,
Boston, Mass. 02108, USA
Set in Baskerville 11/12 pt
and printed in Great Britain by
Unwin Bros Ltd

ISBN 0 7100 8439 0

This book is sponsored by the
Anglo-Jewish Association of
Upper Woburn Place, London WC1

Contents

Contents

Plates

Foreword
by Lord Amory

I feel it a great privilege to be given the opportunity of writing a brief foreword to this book about Sir Basil Henriques.

The life work of Basil and Rose Henriques is a fit subject for a book. It is a story which must appeal to anyone who admires devotion to an ideal, warmth of humanity and utter unselfishness.

Sir Basil was consistent throughout his life. All he did added up and the example he set inspired everyone with whom he came into contact. His personality radiated sympathy with his fellow beings and this quality marked his work on the Magistrates' Bench as well as in the Boys' Club world which he did so much to enrich by his example.

Everyone who believes in voluntary public service will find in the pages of this book a complete confirmation of its value to the nation, illustrated by the lives of two devoted public servants.

Preface

When Basil's widow, my sister Rose Henriques, began to write his life her first and very heavy task was to sort out and put in order the great mass of papers, letters and diaries which he had preserved since childhood. With great courage she worked on through her terminal illness and when she died her book was all but finished. It was, however, unpublishable on account of its immense length, while the chronological method which she employed made it too difficult for me to abridge. I therefore re-wrote it in its present form which I could not have done without the work she did on the papers and the diaries.

The Bernhard Baron St George's Jewish Settlement lived and throve on the work of many devoted people whose names are recorded in its *Fiftieth Anniversary Review* published in 1964; in this book which is meant to be a portrait of Basil I have mentioned only those of them who worked with him so long and intimately as to fit naturally into the picture.

I thank first of all my wife for helping me in every possible way and my two children and Prof. D. P. Walker for reading the typescript and giving me advice; the learned persons who patiently answered my questions; my publishers for keeping my material in order and not least my friend Mrs R. Goble of West Ashling, for her most efficient clerical help, willingly given.

L.L.L.

1

Childhood

Basil Lucas Quixano Henriques was born on 17 October 1890 at 17 Sussex Square, London, the youngest of the five children of David and Agnes Henriques. He writes in one of his diaries:

> My grandfather was born in Jamaica in 1811 and his great-grandfather had died there in 1758 . . . My grandfather was commissioned a lieutenant in a company of artillery in the Kingston Regiment of Foot Militia . . . He was promoted captain in 1846. In 1842 he had been made J.P. and an 'Assistant Judge to the Chief Justice of Jamaica'. In 1845 he came to England and established the firm of D. Q. Henriques & Co., Import and Export Merchants. My grandfather died in 1896 and my father carried on the business.

Be that as it may, it was his great-great-grandfather, born in Kingston in 1740, who founded the family of Quixano Henriques and his great-grandfather was the first of that name to settle in England.[1] From about 1550 onwards some of the Jews who had fled from the Inquisition in Spain and Portugal began to settle in Jamaica; in England some of the founders of the congregation of the Resettlement in 1656 bore the name of Henriques.

Soon after his eighth birthday he began his lifelong habit of keeping a diary; it survives, so that he can tell us about his childhood with his thoughts unchanged by hindsight.

There is nothing very striking about these early diaries, whether by way of humour, originality or charm. They are what one would expect of a nice, intelligent, good-natured child who chose to keep a diary; frank, unselfconscious, very

1

pleased with himself when he does well but never showing-off. These excerpts tell us something about the boy (something else, perhaps, to the psychologist) and give clear indications of how the family lived and the class in which they moved.

The diary, partly dictated and partly written by him, gives the year and the month but not the day of the week except Saturday.

February, 1898.
Saturday. Went to synagogue with father; fog all the morning.
Father went to Norwood meeting. Drove with Mother in afternoon.
School as usual. Wish I could write some things fresh, but can't.
Mother dreadful headache; could not amuse me this evening.
Saturday. Father and I went to synagogue.
Came home with Nana.
Father, Mother and Sybil went to lunch with boys at Harrow.
Went to school. Mr. Box said I was good and did not have to stand up.
March.
School, top of the first division in French.
Tea with Eric; enjoyed myself very much.
School; can't remember.
Saturday. Passover came in. I sat up.
Boat race; Cambridge won.
Came to Sidmouth; dinner on train.
April.
Left Sidmouth and returned to London.
Saturday. I foget.
Went to Albert Hall with Father and Mother.
May.
School. Played cricket for the form.
I am dressed all in white. Swaggered. Looked at self in glass.
School. Played in the Gardens. Boy made my nose bleed.
Saw the Queen; Indian prince waved his hand to me.
Mother's dinner party; I went down to receive.
June.

School. Kept in for laughing.
School and cricket. Boys threw stones at me.
Went to call on Aunt Abby [Mrs Edward Behrens]. Letter
from Aunt Bea [Mrs Francis Samuel].
My report came; good.
School. Done wonderfully well. Rode home on bus.
Doing well in exams; sent in marks to Mother.
September (at the seaside).
I foget.
Day of Atonement. I read prayers all day. Felt very good and
rather dickey.
Returned from Sheringham; commenced school; done well.
Bought my first top hat also a new cap for school.
November.
I forget these days.
I can't do it.

Basil inherited from each of his parents the twofold tradition
of the worship of God and the practice of charity. His
grandfather, Jacob Quixano Henriques, had been a President of
the West London Synagogue of British Jews (familiarly known
as the Reform Synagogue) in Upper Berkeley Street, where
Basil would go every Sabbath with his father, staying longer as
he grew older, happy enough to listen to the hymns and the
organ and getting accustomed to the sound of Hebrew. His
mother's mother, Mrs Philip Lucas, not only read and loved
the Bible but filled her copy of it with intelligent commentary;
this became Basil's first Bible and he kept it all his life. His first
prayers were said at his mother's knee and all his life, contrary
to Jewish custom, he said his private prayers on his knees. 'The
essentials of Judaism, which I have attempted to spread among
my co-religionists, were taught to me by my mother; the
Mission of Israel, the sanctity of the Sabbath, the value of
prayer, the true place of ceremonialism in religion, and above
all, the appeal to the indwelling Spirit of God as the final arbiter
of all action.'[2] It is impossible to over-estimate the lasting
effect of the early religious and ethical teaching by his
parents.

The 'meeting' was of the Committee of what was then called
the Jews' Hospital and Orphan Asylum and is now the

Norwood Homes for Jewish Children, on which Basil in his turn served as a committee-man for forty-seven years.

Sybil, then sixteen and beautiful, was his only sister, and he loved her dearly all his life. His three brothers Julian, Ronald and Harold were all at Harrow.

'School' was Mr Wilkinson's Preparatory School overlooking Kensington Gardens. (Could it have been 'Pilkington's', whose shade, says Barrie, was over all Kensington Gardens?) Basil was very happy there.

As for laughing in class his detention was in vain. He was born with a sense of the absurd at which he could giggle like a child.

So far the entries show him as a townsman; we may as well have a glimpse of him as a country gentleman when they are all staying with his Aunt Abby at her house in Bettisfield.

January 1899.
Saturday. Read prayers with Sybil. Lovely day. Saw the hunters off. Got 21 eggs; whipped Katie's ponies about. [His cousin, Katie Behrens.]
Lovely day; covert shooting; 3 extra gentlemen.
Saturday. Poured all day. There was a meet in the Park. I ran after them to the Lodge. Calf born at 2 o'clock.
Caddied for a 4-some—Sybil and Harold against Julian and Ronald. Went for walk with Katie; 3 pigs were killed, saw their blood.
Julian went shooting and got a brace; evening Sybil put her hair up.

In the nursery there was the game of sermons. Standing on a footstool and using the back of a chair as a pulpit Basil would preach a sermon to Nana and his brothers who had to sit demurely in a row facing him; such were the rules of the game. Two of the 'sermons' survive, written in a very small note-book, together with the examination results of his whole class in every subject. Here is one of them.

'On being kind to the poor'
We all know that we can show our goodness in different ways. There is only one person who is always with us and

that is God. Now we know that there is a God and let us now try and see what we can do to please Him. We must pray to Him and He will grant peace to us, we must not speak evil and He will guide us.

My Brethren we must turn from the good to the wrong you will say to do wrong to God is to speak evil.
Well it is that but that is not the chief thing. The chief thing is not to speak or teach evil to the poor and if we do not fear God how are we to think that God will help us. He need not think we are the only people (when I say 'we' I mean the gentleman and richer) who know that there is a God the poor know they pray just as much in a way. Well you are aware a Clergeman has to teach the poor and help them, that is how the poor know that there is a God. Do you know that this is the greatest kindness that there is, because when the poor goeth home he will pray to God and God will listen to him, will make him prosper.

Let us try to good like the Clerge-man for it is not only the Clerge-man who does but other people if we trust in the Lord and wait patiently for him we will prosper.

It is perhaps not very exceptional for little boys to play at preaching sermons not much better or worse than this until they grow out of it, but Basil was to go on preaching sermons for the rest of his life, some very good, none of them said to be bad.

When he was about eleven he left Wilkinson's with a good report and went to a boarding school at Elstree. It was a time when life must have been full of fun for a boy; preparations for the Coronation of Edward VII, troops for the Boer war coming and going, processions everywhere. He was happy enough as a boarder; he writes to his mother:

Dearest,
    I was so pleased with your long letter full of news that I must try and write the same in mine . . . There is an Indian Prince, or at least his father is a Raja Secertry, in other words King of all the Indian Secertrys. He is now sitting with me as he does not go to Chaple it is aufuly funny he has an Indian servant comes and looks after him. He also sleeps in the same

5

Dorm as me. Good lummy!! he has just come in speaking broken English to me and can't understand. I am aufuly happy and so you are not to worry. The Indian is now being kissed. I can't help laughing. Yes I have got my remove and am now in the second form. I am allowed to play goal as my nikers are not finished yet. What I really want for my birthday is a real nice engine about £4 and I want you all to join together Sybil, Mother, Father and the boys and also a hamper. With best love from Basil.

He did not get his engine; he was not spoilt. Instead his mother had something to say about his spelling and, as usual, told him a great deal about what was going on, the war, politics, and so on. These 'written conversations' persisted until manhood. His mind must have been well stocked with general knowledge; perhaps that is why he twice got a prize for his diaries. He kept a voluminous one during a holiday in Switzerland in the summer of 1902; it shows a boyish, fresh pleasure in landscape, pictures, music and buildings. He had, in fact, an eye and an ear for beautiful things and never lost either of them. His father writes to him: 'It is a pleasure to take you abroad because you remember what you see.'

There is another diary of three weeks' holiday-time in Swanage and London when he was eleven. He describes everything in great detail: his visits to Corfe Castle, to churches, to caves, to villages; in London the Zoo, the British Museum, the National Gallery, the theatre. His reactions to such a variety of stimuli sound happy but dutiful. Spelling mistakes are underlined, as if in a holiday-task, while his comments have more than a faint echo of his elders.

'Cuyp, the wonderful landscape painter', 'Gainsborough, what a magnificent painter'. 'There is a magnificent old arch, quite Norman ... round the arch are calvings (sic) called "Dog's teeth" ', ' "The Country Girl" at Daly's was most amusing; Huntly Wright was the making of the peace.' Once, however, he breaks through the culture-barrier. On the boat back to Swanage 'the sea became quite rough. I stayed in the bow of the ship the whole day getting splashed with waves. I enjoyed my day very much.'

When he left Elstree in 1902 as 'Top Boy' his report was

'Good sound capable work without being brilliant. He is a boy of good taste, not without a sense of humour. I shall miss him dreadfully.'

He was next sent to another boarding school at Lockers Park in Surrey, perhaps to improve his chances of getting into Harrow. No diary is extant; from his letters life appears to have been happy but uneventful but for the first appearance of certain imperfectly diagnosed symptoms, referred to vaguely as 'digestive troubles'. Perhaps nowadays they would be called psychosomatic. He was beginning to show signs of a diffidence and anxiety about his progress which haunted him until he came down from Oxford and until that time the symptoms intermittently continued.

2

Harrow and Oxford

Basil's schooldays at Harrow were spent in a losing battle against ill-health. From time to time the undiagnosed maladies returned. He had become a highly strung adolescent with a very sensitive conscience, oppressed by a feeling of guilt and shame if he failed or fell short. Yet he was liking Harrow and enjoying his schooldays. He entered with ardour into school activities: cricket, squash, the cadet corps and music (though he didn't like being made to sing), at all of which he was at least a good trier. His work varied, but was never below average. His letters show him happy enough, but always there is an obsessive anxiety about his chances of 'doing well', perhaps for his parents' sake. In October 1904 he wrote to his mother:

> I have some news which may interest you. The news is that I have had a Greek prose sent up. I got 46 marks out of 50 with Ex [for excellent] written on it. I think it will be accepted but I'm not sure about the French prose . . . I am getting into the ways of Harrow now. I sometimes have a lot of work to do in the evenings but I am beginning to see how and when to do it. I hate 'Bill' and always shall [Bill was a form of muster or assembly] . . . I think Mr. Somervell [housemaster] is very kind but very like mother. He has given me jaw in a very motherly manner. If you can't do your con. he is awfully kind in going over it with you and will go on explaining it to you for a long time.

Good for Harrow! It appears, however, that there was an illicit custom of using cribs, which may have accounted for the giving of jaw.

'I have had tea', he writes, 'with Mr. Golly. He is really extremely kind and I am sorry for him when they rag him so.' 'Golly' was Israel Gollancz, the Shakespearian scholar who taught religion to the Jewish Harrovians. It was partly to his friendly guidance that Basil owed discrimination in his choice of reading matter and style in his essay-writing. Under him, too, Basil first read *The Bible for Home Reading* by C. G. Montefiore.[1] There was to be a life-long friendship and correspondence between him and C. G. M.

A letter written after the summer holidays shows signs of a little rebelliousness:

> Now that last holidays are over I feel how at times I must have hurt you both by my foolish manner, but you are a forgiving parent and know how I was conquered in trying to conquer, and that I shall think of my weak points, as I did on the Day of Atonement and see if I can be the Conqueror of the Devil next 12 months. I was delighted with the hamper.

He did well in October and got a double remove into the top class of the Lower School; the work was difficult and he was ill again in December. Next year he got the Headmaster's prize for an essay on Hamlet, in which his mother thought she saw the hand of Gollancz. Early in 1907 there was a falling off (his housemaster said there were good reasons for it; among other things he had grown inordinately tall), and in April it was decided that he should leave Harrow temporarily until he completely recovered his health. Francis Storrs, son of the Dean of Rochester, was engaged as his tutor and became his good friend. A visit to the seaside was followed by a sea voyage to the Mediterranean with a school friend whose parents had invited Basil to make the trip with them. In July 1907, feeling very much better, he went back to Harrow to finish the term. Mr Somervell, describing him to a tutor, said, 'you will find him a pleasant, intelligent, high-principled boy, full of life and spirit, a pleasant companion and a willing worker. I know nothing but good about him.' However, it became clear that the strain would be too much for him and he left the school at the end of the summer term, 1907, having borne, as his headmaster said 'an excellent character'.

The educational gap was happily filled. French was taught at

Harrow by a Monsieur Minssen whose mother had a house in Versailles where she used to accept Harrovians to be coached by her daughters, two accomplished and good-natured Lycéennes, Marguerite and Marie, who were Heads of Department at the Versailles Lycée, and there Basil went. He wrote, 'The house is very quaint and old-fashioned, full of mysterious doors which seem to turn into long passages . . . Marguerite and Marie were there with their dear old mother . . . Mlle. Marie is "charmante". She is quite pretty and is always full of fun and jokes . . . I am going to be very happy here.' Perhaps he was happy because he had finished with what might nowadays be called the rat-race or tensions of school life. He did not have to measure up to anybody else's standards: he set his own, by which Marie judged him. There seem to have been no set hours and teaching went on all day. 'They pounce on one dreadfully if you make a mistake . . . They are very nice and repeat the thing over and over again. I do not get cross about it.' Remote control was still in operation from Sussex Square. 'I want to know more exactly how your time is filled up; send me a plan to see', wrote his father on his seventeenth birthday; furthermore he had already made 'the 4 o'clock rule' under which Basil must never be in Paris alone after that time; this irked him because he had to refuse dinner invitations from relatives and friends passing through Paris.

Nevertheless, it was a happy time. Marie showed him Paris and Versailles, while his work, in addition to some classics, mathematics and music, consisted in a sort of junior 'Greats' course in the form of essay-writing on the widest variety of subjects: art, history, literature, ethics, politics and what not. The essays would be carefully discussed, criticised and assessed by Marie. It was as well that she did so because he was threatened with a graver danger than that which his father feared for him after dark in Paris. His letters show that he was in danger of becoming a prig and a sentimentalist. English humour is 'low', French humour is 'repulsive'. *The Mikado* is 'clownish buffoonery'; in an essay on Westminster Abbey he says: 'I have no need of dates, no desire to see the tombs of great men. I am in a delirium of lofty thought; my mind is full of One Great King, for am I not in his holy presence?' That he never became either a prig or a sentimentalist was due partly to the sagacity and common sense of his parents who had occasion to tell him of his 'fresh and uncritical mind' and partly to the clear and perceptive mind of Marie Minssen.

Marie's part in these events reveals a nobility of character which goes far to relieve their sadness. There grew up between them a 'sympathie réciproque' as she calls it, which became a very affectionate friendship. He poured out to her all his introspections described by her as his complexities, difficulties, obstacles and frustrations, his moral and intellectual isolation. It must be said on his behalf that he was an emotional, sensitive adolescent and that the solid virtues of the life he was expected to lead, not to be undervalued because they were socially respectable, did not satisfy certain undefined ideals and aspirations which were beginning to be urgent and were to become over-mastering. She, for her part, was his tutor and she played the game. She reminded him that he was seventeen and she forty-one; 'il y a chez toute femme une maman berceuse' and on that footing they discuss everything 'sans timidité et fausse honte'. She tells him, in the kindest terms, not to be morbid and to avoid aimless meditation and to go on trying not to blame everybody but himself for all his difficulties. Above all, 'Vivez de toute votre force; c'est le moment.'

Soon after he left she fell ill and died within a year. Her long letters to him, affectionate but without 'tutoiement', show the serenity with which she bore great suffering. In a farewell letter she says their friendship has been 'noble, haute et pure'. Her last words to him are in English: 'Be yourself, dear, dear Basil.' It was his first acquaintance with grief.

During the Versailles period Basil did not forget his Judaism, and re-arranged his classes so that he could go to synagogue in Paris. Occasionally a social conscience asserted itself, so that he reproachfully compared the frugality of the Minssen children with the luxurious life of his small nephews. Sometimes the old pains returned but the specialist assured his father, without precisely diagnosing the trouble, that in due course it would vanish for ever, and so it did.

The summer of 1908 and the following spring were spent partly in Versailles, partly at a crammer's in Tonbridge where, he said, he felt 'like a monkey in a cage but the food is tip-top'. The immediate objective was such examination results as would get him into Oxford and accepted by New College. His crammer called him 'one of the best' and said he wished he had twenty pupils like him. Of course, the spectre of examinations made him occasionally gloomy, anxious and ill, but when well and not working he was the young man about town: Carreño at Queen's Hall with dinner at Gatti's, taxi to the Boat Race and dinner at the 'Cri', The Follies (where he meets Storrs), golf at Folkestone, 'sumptuous lunch' at Calais on a day trip with his father, visit to the House of Commons with tea at the Carlton, shopping with his mother in the afternoon and Bauer playing Beethoven in the evening. He had a look at Cambridge ('so as to compare my first impressions of each university') and found the city 'chill and unartistic' but spent a few hours playing roulette in a friend's rooms and losing £4. He tried his first cigar.

Eventually, after a failure at New College which threw him into despair, he got in at University College. No more pains, at least for the time being; lunch at the Eton and Harrow match, a visit from the Minssens and general congratulations.

Oxford

When Basil went up to Oxford he did not know what he wanted to do or to be. He had learnt from experience that there were certain things to which he could not or would not apply his mind successfully and that the fear of failure made him ill; he was also to learn that among them was the study of history, which he had decided to read for a degree. By the time he went down he knew very well what he could do and the sort of life he wanted to lead. His progress from Doubting Castle to the Delectable Mountain is all that really matters in the story of his undergraduate days, together with a short account of what has facetiously been called his 'Mission to the Jews of Oxford'.

He had a good start. He found a few old friends at the college, he liked and was liked by the Master (Dr Macan) and the Dean (Dr Farquarson) and he was lucky to get rooms in college in his second term, at which period, January 1910, the Dean told his parents: 'his work does not seem congenial to him, but he is a nice fellow and I have a real liking for him.'

12

In those days, while a minority of undergraduates were professed agnostics or atheists, most of them cared about religion more or less; some cared very much and, like Basil, were sorting out their beliefs, girding against established ideas and practices. It is therefore not surprising that he should have gone to hear the Bishop of London preach, about which he wrote home: 'He is most convincing, with his charming manners. He is not a great man, but he is likely to do an immense amount of good in the world.' Basil was beginning to be preoccupied with 'doing good in the world'. He asked his parents for more information about the new religious movement called 'Liberal Judaism' launched by Dr Montefiore (whose *Bible for Home Reading* he had read at Harrow). He told them that he agreed neither with the orthodox nor with the reformed service: 'I suppose the world of Jewry is not yet ready or willing to receive a service reformed in bending the knee in prayer, removing the hat in synagogue, praying chiefly in our modern language and retaining the Hebrew for tradition only. We want reform, even more violent reform than your service gives us.' He compared Judaism unfavourably with Christianity; the teachings of Jesus, he said, are the foundations of our civilisation and social justice. The sharing of suffering and sorrow, going out among the poor, these are the teachings of the Perfect Man. Jewish ministers, on the other hand, never speak from their heart to his, never speak to him of God the creator, or of life as it should be led, or of the teachings of Jesus. His mother told him, in effect, that when he knows more he will think differently; she compared his 'dawn of thought' with the mature outlook of the ministers. Furthermore she had views on sermons which she expressed with heroic impartiality. She wrote (5 May 1910): 'On Sunday we went to Canterbury Cathedral for service. Talk of our sermons being poor! The one we heard was worse than any at Upper Berkeley Street. Go and listen to sermons in churches; you will discover they are little or no better than ours.' And she knew how and when to be terse, thus, 'I wrote for the books you want me to read; Oscar Wilde is not in the circulating library.'

Of his new history tutor, Mr Kenneth Leys, he said (in *Indiscretions of a Warden*): 'I used to go to Leys at 9 p.m. and seldom left him until 1 a.m. My private hours with him were a joy to which I looked forward each week. He was the Oxford representative of Toynbee Hall . . . He succeeded in rousing my interest in political economy, social science and constitutional history, and made me think things out for myself. Social questions became a living problem and he made me try to work out the causes and cure of poverty.'

He had been brought up as a Liberal, but in the Whig rather than the radical wing of a party then large enough to comprehend both. In 1910 his mother wrote to him: 'Don't be a Socialist, our strength as an Empire has been that of unity, but Socialism will be its downfall. Advance with the Liberalism of the times, but don't go further.'

By 1912 the Leysian yeast seems to have been working. His father wrote: 'You ask "Wasn't Lloyd-G excellent in the city?". My answer is that . . . he did not diminish the feeling of mistrust caused by his rapid violent and ill-considered course of ultra-socialism.' The speech was a defence of the increased expenditure incurred in financing Old Age Pensions and National Insurance. The 'feeling of mistrust' had shown itself in a twelve-point fall in Consols.

In his second year, after meeting the Bishops of London and Oxford and hearing them talk of social work in East London, he startled his parents by announcing that unless they objected he proposed spending a week of the Easter vacation at Oxford House,[2] Bethnal Green. Shortly afterwards he met Barclay Baron, Warden of the Oxford and Bermondsey Mission.[3] This meeting, and a subsequent one with Alec Paterson (whose Across the Bridges Basil had read) were climacteric. 'We talked till 2.30 a.m. and discussed the possibility of running a Jewish Mission on the lines of the Oxford and Bermondsey Mission . . . You can organise for the poor pleasant little social evenings . . . and keep them thus from temptations and evils . . . It is not sufficient to do a negative thing. We must, to be successful, give them something more than they came with.' (Nearly forty years later, when Paterson died, Basil wrote: 'He was the greatest inspiration of my life'.) To his parents' reasonable protest that degree work should come before social work he wrote: 'Can't you see that before me I see a path which leads to something more beautiful than death and that I have ideals? When may I give away to others who have not, all that wealth and education have given me? You will not stop me from doing the only unselfish act of my life?' Finally the parents agreed; in fact it was his mother who persuaded him that foreign Jews and their children could be 'anglicised' into being members of a Jewish Boys' Club.

After spending a few days with the residents of the Oxford and Bermondsey Mission he wrote home:

> I don't think I can ever thank you sufficiently for allowing me to go to Bermondsey. You can have no idea what these few days have done to me; how happy they have made me in opening my eyes to a future so full of wonderful opportunities. I don't think I shall ever wonder again whether life is worth living, for my whole outlook has been changed by the many people of whom I was totally ignorant but whom I am now just beginning to know and love.

He soon got some 'field work' to do, and went over to France with a senior boy of the Bermondsey Mission to survey a camp site. An entry in his diary at that time shows that he was envisaging a life in the manner of St Francis: 'If I am to go among the lowest dregs of society, the down and outs, the prostitutes and the criminals, and share my life with them, I know I must do so as their equal, their Brother.'

The services of the Oxford Hebrew Congregation were held in the traditional manner so that those members who were in the reform movement or who did not know Hebrew stayed away. Basil wrote: 'The general Jewish war cry up here is—what on earth's the good of going to synagogue if you can't understand a syllable?—I hope I shall live to see bare heads and bent knees. I should then have realised my ideal creed and worship.' He never quite understood how much some people might be affronted by such suggestions.

He tells us about his plans:

> I am going to bring in a very big reform and hope to get an endowment for a resident minister which will mean at least £10,000 . . . I simply long to achieve my object which is to make religion an attractive reality among the Jews up here. At present it is far from being a reality or in the smallest degree attractive.

A group outlined the plan in a letter to the *Jewish Chronicle* in which the case as between the different sectaries was fairly stated: one of the signatories was Neville Laski (later Judge Laski, QC).

The plan failed, partly for lack of undergraduate support. But Basil pressed on; he was elected honorary secretary of the congregation and a revised form of service for the Sabbath Eve was tried out, read by him. It was a success, and ultimately a compromise was arrived at whereby part of the service was read in English and part in Hebrew, while some 'Liberal' prayers were included. A new congregational prayer book was devised for which Basil and Henry Alexander of Queen's were responsible. Finally his Aunt Alice gave a cover for the reading desk 'with sincere wishes that the service may be established for the honour of true worship'. Poor Aunt Alice! About fifty years later her nephew was saying: 'The Synagogue is a disgrace to the Community . . . Cobwebs on the candlesticks. It looks altogether uncared for.'[4]

In the meantime, Basil had been at work at the centre of things. He and C. G. M. and the Chief Rabbi had moved some of the lay leaders of the Jewish Community to endow an academic post at Oxford independently of the Oxford Hebrew Congregation but with a gentleman's agreement that the holder would act as guide, philosopher and friend to that body. At that time a lectureship in Hebrew at St Catharine's College, Cambridge, was held by Herbert Loewe, an orientalist whom Basil had met and liked, and in 1913 he accepted the offer of the Oxford post. Writing to Basil two years later he says that he found warmth and friendship among the Oxford congregation 'but the spiritual revival is due to you'.[5]

But his life was not wholly spent in an agony of the spirit and religious polemics. On the contrary, when he was well and not working he was enjoying the very enviable life of a nice rich young man with nice rich young friends: jaunts to London; river picnics, dinners and dances, concerts where Pachmann, Paderewski, Carreño and Casals played; he was invited to a ball at Blenheim to meet the ex-King of Portugal, though he never knew why; did they search the residents' lists for an Iberian name? Anyway, he enjoyed it enormously and stayed till 4 a.m. He does not seem to have played any games except golf, which he gave up in favour of walks. He certainly did not stint himself. His mother wrote (31 January 1912): 'Do tell me why you are at the very beginning of term crying not poverty but really starvation? . . . You have no idea how this constant cry or want of money distresses us. Father gives you ample but with your own extra money you are no better off than you were . . . You should retrench.'

In the vacations there were reading parties in the Cotswolds, walking parties in the Lakes and on Exmoor, expeditions with friends to France, Germany, Switzerland and Italy—'at Florence my heart really swelled and I had to gasp for breath, it was so beautiful'. He was a member of the Gridiron and of the 'Martlets' to whom he read a paper on the poet Drummond which was well received by a fairly learned audience.

It was soon to end. In the long vacation of 1912 he was walking on Exmoor with a party of friends, very happy and carefree. He suddenly felt that he must go home. He did not know why, and could only make excuses. He arrived home that evening to find his parents well and in good spirits. His father died early next morning of heart failure.

The shock of his father's death, his longing to be at work with the Mission, and the long campaign for reform in the synagogue had kept his mind away from work. In November 1913 he wrote to his brother Ronald, then with his regiment in the West Indies:

> If only when I have put my books away I could work out historical problems in my head . . . I should still say there was hope, but I can't and don't. History, dates, battles, foreign policies, impeachments, attainders . . . one great blur in my head and all rolling about on top of each other.

In the Christmas vacation he had to have a long and painful controversy with his family before he could wear down their opposition to his making a career in social service. Fear of failure in his schools made him ill; the doctors forbade him to go back to Oxford and ordered a sea voyage, so he went out to Bermuda to see Ronald. He came back to Oxford in the beginning of April, earlier than was expected, and worked as much as the doctors would let him. It was a gallant effort and it was just enough; he got a degree and became a free man.

When he went down he spent a week in camp with a Jewish boys' club, and then went on a round of visits to family and friends, including a few days with C. G. M. in his country house in Hampshire. In September there was the walking tour, planned long since with his friend Ralph Wigram, in the Tyrol and the Dolomites, and if it was something of a sentimental journey it seems to have done them both a great deal of good.

> Never have I felt my brain so clear, so clean, so hungry and so healthy. I began after this week of absolute mental rest to look forward to work and worry again. Physically I felt strong enough to stand anything. Morally I felt at peace. The scenery had spoken to me as God's Holy Messenger. This holiday with my dear old Ralph will be good for me, when I hunger, for many a long day . . . We talked of all that was closest to us, of God, of man, of marriage, love and hatred; of oppression, misery, and sorrow, of joy and happiness; of death and of life . . . We made ambitious ideals; we were determined after higher things. What will become of these dreams? Shall we, if we live, laugh at them in our grey hairs, or shall we cherish them as the nucleus of a future life. Whatever happens in the future those talks were worth the talking, for I loved them; they made me happier than I have been for years.

In this frame of mind he came back to London to begin his life's work; in his own words, to serve God by serving men.

3

Apprenticeship

When Basil came to the East End to serve his apprenticeship in boys' club work there were plenty of good masters, Christian and Jewish, for a willing pupil. There were thirty-nine clubs in the London Federation of Boys' Clubs and the great John Stansfeld—'The Doctor'—of the Oxford Medical Mission, now a canon of the Church of England, one of the greatest names in boys' club work and a legendary figure—was still around; Basil was lucky to meet him.

Six of the clubs were Jewish and among those who founded them were the pioneers of the Jewish youth movement.

There was a need for such people. When his mother had encouraged him to 'anglicise' the East End Jews the expression still meant something. Throughout a century of persecution, pogroms and mass expulsions, emigration had brought from the Slavonic countries to East London about 120,000 Russo-Polish Jews, most of whom had arrived destitute and speaking no English. About half of them lived in and around Stepney. Treating them as a communal problem the *Jewish Chronicle* said in 1881:[1]

> They retain all the habits of their former home and display no desire to assimilate with the people among whom they dwell . . . They join a Chevra,[2] mix only with their fellow-countrymen and do in England as the Poles do . . . By improving their dwellings, attracting them to our synagogues, breaking down their isolation in all directions and educating their children in an English fashion one can do much to change our foreign poor into brethren, who shall not only be Jews but English Jews.

The first to use a youth club to this end was the Hon. Lily Montagu, who founded the West Central Jewish Girls' Club in 1893; two years later Col. Goldsmid, Ernest Joseph and others built up the Jewish Lads' Brigade which produced 'a number of notably virile, strongly self-disciplined boys' (W. McG. Eagar, in *Making Men*).

Brady Street Club was founded in 1896 by A. Lesser and Victoria Boys' Club in 1901 by Charles Sebag-Montefiore, who had long remained a boy at heart, having played in all four fifteens of the Wasps Rugby Football Club, graduating up to the first, and then, when age slowed him up, down again to the fourth. Both he and Lesser served on the committee of the London Federation. About the same time members of the East London Synagogue, led by the Rev. J. F. Stern, set up the Stepney Jewish Lads' Club, three of whose managers, Gerald Samuel, Denzil Myer and Leonard Stern, were killed in the First World War. Hutchison House, the West Central Jewish Lads' Club and the Notting Hill Boys' Club soon followed.

This was the framework of youth clubs in which Basil found himself when he was granted residence in Toynbee Hall,[3] Commercial Street, Whitechapel.

He arrived on 29 September 1913 and was immediately handed over to Mrs Willis, the honorary secretary of the Charity Organisation Society,[4] under whom he settled down to do case-work. His diary shows him eager, almost greedy for work. Besides telling us about himself and how he lived he gives the details of many of his cases. For the case-worker they were the run of the mill but they give us a vivid picture of poverty in Stepney before the Welfare State.

Writing in 1961 on the club movement he said: 'During nearly half a century of club life I have seen some almost unbelievable external, material changes in the environment of club members. Starvation and poverty existed in those days; overcrowding in the vast area of slums was appalling; sickness or unemployment of the wage-earners meant ruination in the family.'

The pattern of his life at this period had three main strands, his pupillage in welfare work, his ambition to create his own club, and his links with his old life and background. Apart from the usefulness of rich relatives and friends when it came to raising money or lobbying for a good cause, he wanted to bring into his club as managers, workers or visitors a classless set of people which should include the sort of men and women he had grown up with. Moreover, he neither was nor purported to be an ascetic. We find him occasionally at a theatre or a dance or a dinner party ('sumptuous dinner with ten courses ... I thoroughly enjoyed the evening'), or lunching at the Reform, and very often visiting or staying with his mother in Sussex Square. The diary entries also show from time to time a self-confidence, perhaps an over-self-confidence, in making judgments on matters of welfare work which his mother might have ascribed to the 'dawn of thought'.

29 September. Visited G. S. dreadfully ill with rheumatic fever and hopelessly weak heart. Looked a charming boy, and most respectable and nice mother. Although he can't move an inch in bed he shares it with a brother. Wants a water-bed which C.O.S. is trying to get him.

Also saw boy with weak heart. Mother and children live in a room 10 ft by 8 ft. Rent 2/-d. Went to West Central Club and ran with the boys. They do not take enough physical exercise. Their conversation is not up to Club standard. Must try and get rid of P [a club leader].

Dined down in Bermondsey and went for a run over the Tower and London Bridges with the Dockland Club. Thoroughly enjoyed my evening. Saw Alec Paterson and Jess Skilton who is waiter at the Cavendish.

1 October. Went to visit H. who is in the advanced stages of consumption. Robin Montefiore[5] came to see me to make arrangements for coming down. Lunched at Lady Sutherland's with Lady Bullock and Evelyn,[6] and afterwards went to see *Joseph and his Brethren* at His Majesty's. It is one of the most impressive and beautiful plays which I have seen.

2 October. New Year's Day [by the Jewish Calendar]. Went to Synagogue with Harold. Robin came to dinner at Bermondsey: we went to several clubs and went to see G. T. . . . . He is now dying of galloping consumption in the throat and is unable to speak. He cannot live more than 2 or 3 weeks. I had to keep talking all the time and the poor lad

could only make signs to show that he understood.

He meets Father 'Dick' Wilson, founder of the 'White House', a home for the destitute, and of the 'Blue House' where factory girls could cook their meals. The latter was a great help. The girls worked twelve hours a day—sometimes doing overtime—with an hour's interval for dinner and half an hour for tea, and few of them would get cooking facilities at their place of work since the Truck Acts prescribed the conditions under which alone an employer could charge for them by way of reduced wages. 'I was charmed by his forcible and kindly personality.' He hears Canon Stansfeld taking prayers in the Dockland Club: 'I was struck by his vivid personality and the hold he had over boys.' He visits Lily Montagu in Kensington Palace Gardens. She was the daughter of the first Lord Swaythling and besides creating a working girls' club was a lay preacher and one of the founding members of the Liberal Jewish Synagogue:

> I have seldom met anyone with such a quiet and yet tremendously powerful personality. She seemed inspired by religion as few are. She was delightfully sympathetic about the club scheme and gave me many valuable hints about the religious question and was in entire agreement with me about the lines on which I want the club to be run. I have seldom left anyone's presence with the same feeling of encouragement and inspiration.
> 2. Went to synagogue [Liberal] with mother where C. G. M. was at his best. Dined at Toynbee. Visited Mrs W. to find out why she asked for free dinners. It was the most awful case I have yet had to deal with. She was in her small but fairly clean and tidy room with her two children, both naked except for a vest. She had had to pawn their clothes to pay the rent . . . Yesterday they had nothing to eat at all. I promised to bring them a loaf of bread, whereupon she fell on her knees in tears and kissed my hand. Went to the West Central Club in the evening. I was extremely annoyed at the indolence and selfishness of the seniors. There is no esprit de corps in this club. Everybody, especially the elders, seem to come to enjoy themselves. As senior committee man I threatened to expel from the club those who did not do

more for it.

7. Did several Care Committee cases.

Basil gives an account of Care Committees in *The Home-Menders* at p. 67. They existed in London only and worked under the direction of the District Child-Care Organiser of the Department of Education of what was then the London County Council and were attached to schools. Their main function was to be a link between the medical inspectorate and the child's parents, taking 'care' that the treatment ordered was properly carried out in cases where the parents could or would not take it themselves. 'Perhaps', he says, 'because they are . . . obviously doing this work out of the goodness of their hearts, they are welcomed in the home and generally become the staunch friends of the family. Many of them are doing most excellent preventive and constructive work.' In 1970 they were disbanded and their members invited to work in 'teams' led by professionals.

He had begun to work with them in the days before the offensive expression 'middle-class do-gooders' was spread abroad and applied to Care Committees by some of those who thought, or at least hoped that a diploma in sociology would be a guarantee of efficient welfare work. Yet the Bedford Report (*An Enquiry into the Social Welfare Services of the Inner London Education Authority 1965-66*) which was by no means uncritical of the Committees had had to record that many heads of schools acknowledged their usefulness (para. 205). In a wider context the Seebohm Committee's report (1968, Cmd. no. 3703, para. 569) spoke of the increasing readiness to co-operate with the voluntary bodies and to make use of their enthusiasm and abilities.

Went to see Miss Ida Samuel at Fairclough Street School. We discussed several cases, and I was struck by her knowledge of the people. Went to Berner St. and Christian St. Schools. The headmaster of Christian St. gave me enthusiastic support for my club. He says it is a crying need; the evils of the district are an appalling temptation.

Care Committee meeting in Fairclough Street. Met Miss Hyam who attracted me. Also Mrs. Matthews, wife of the

L.C.C. member . . . we went through a tremendous number of cases.

Miss Samuel, a very experienced social worker, was related to Basil by marriage.

Miss Hyam worked as a Care Committee member at the Bernhard Baron Settlement for twenty-five years: her great services and lovable nature are commemorated in annual Hannah Hyam Lectures, of which the first was by Dame Myra Curtis, CBE, on 'The Deprived Child'.

9. Took Robin round Care Committee visiting . . . We saw a place in Cannon St. Road belonging to the Raine's Trust which except for its size and expense is ideal for club premises. I was so excited about it that I went to get C. G. M. who was at the Jews' Infant School in Commercial Road. I rather lost my head about it because in a cooler moment I realised that it was much too large and far too expensive.

Visited C.O.S. cases and then went home and dined with Sybil. Meeting at Liberal Jewish Synagogue to discuss the St. George's Club . . . They were enthusiastic about it before we left, but doubtful about the money. I am asking for £300 for the first year . . . The whole scheme is to be reported to the Council.

11. Went to Berkeley Street Synagogue on the Day of Atonement until 2.30, and as I wore a skull cap I did not get a headache. I had a terrific struggle with myself about someone who had said something that hurt me dreadfully. I was deeply impressed by the service this year. Later I took Mother to Hill Street [the Liberal Synagogue] and thought the service most beautiful. I have never known a Day of Atonement have such a repenting effect on me before . . . It really seemed that God had heard my prayers at once. That struggle was a wonderful one. I shall remember it as one of the great experiences of my life.

12. Went to see Sybil and then lunched with Mattuck [the rabbi of the Liberal Synagogue] . . . he thinks that the Council of Hill Street will look kindly towards the club proposals. Went to the Albert Hall with Robin where Carreño was playing. She was very charming to me when I

went to see her in the Artists' Room. Afterwards went for
the Care Committee to see Mrs. H. She works until 8.30
every night and the children seem terribly neglected. Went
on afterwards to Victoria Boys' Club. This seems to be much
better managed though far from ideal. Charles
Sebag-Montefiore took us round. They have excellent
systems to encourage economy and industry . . . but the club
seemed too big to be properly managed, i.e. individual
attention to each boy . . . Their camp seems to be managed
on superb lines.
18. Went for a walk in the Park with Sybil and then did some
shopping. Saw Stein[7] at Toynbee about the club. He quite
rightly advises me to get guarantees for at least £200 a year
for 4 years and also to demand a large marginal sum as capital
outlay.

Harold [a brother] dined me at the Bath Club and we
went to see Mrs. Horniman's company in *Hindle Wakes* at
the Court. This play was banned at Oxford this year. It is
most interesting, offering much food for thought.

I found Father Embling at St. Saviour's College. We had a
long talk before dinner and tried to find out how nearly our
two religions met. I think he was astonished to learn how
personal and spiritual Judaism is. I dined with 'The Brethren'
and then Father Hugh and I set out to visit a dosshouse, i.e. a
common[8] lodging house at 5d a night. We just saw the
dormitories, which hold about 60 beds each. There are 10 of
these, and except for the fact that the sheets were only
washed once a week, they looked quite comfortable. Then
we descended downstairs into the huge half-dozen white
tiled halls, simply packed with the miserable scum of the
earth. In each hall there was a magnificent roaring fire,
before which some men were cooking fish and others were
warming themselves, whilst others again were drying the few
and only clothes they possessed, which they had been
allowed to wash in the tubs supplied for the purpose . . . We
talked to one or two. One chap was making artificial flowers
out of papers with real delicate taste. Another was glueing
together pieces of boxwood and contrived from these some
really excellent 'dogs huts' to sell in the street. We were told
that of these 600 men nearly 50% were old soldiers. An

appalling percentage . . . I went back to the college for
evening prayers which were most impressive.

I went down to see Denzil Myer's club [the Stepney
Jewish Lads' Club] at Stepney. It is far and away the best
Jewish club I have visited. Charmingly simple, comfortable
and non-luxurious, and a splendid spirit among the boys.

Sybil and Mrs. Horn [mother of a Harrovian friend] came
down to see St. George's. The Head Teachers were most kind
in showing us as much as possible.

Went up to Oxford. Went to see Leys first, and then Claud
Lucas who has my old room . . . I went to Synagogue.
Perhaps here more than ever I found the true inspiration of
life, the greatness of it; the opportunities it affords; the
smallness of us. I was very happy indeed when I was asked to
read the service, and felt more with God than I have for some
time. Charming letter from Clive Behrens with a very
handsome cheque for the club.

17. Ernest Joseph and I met the Raines Governors and went
into the question of rent, etc. for the premises in Cannon
Street Road . . . Was at the Jewish Board of Guardians most
of the afternoon discussing cases. Mr. S. [on the staff of the
board] struck me as a most kind and sympathetic old man.

The Jewish Board of Guardians had been founded in 1850
for the purpose of looking after the Jewish poor in the London
area. Its offices were then in Houndsditch and its work was of
more than marginal importance to Jewish youth clubs. It is
now the Jewish Welfare Board.

On another occasion:

One fellow was refused help altogether (for very good
reasons) and used the most awful language to us. It needed
two huge men to show him the door . . . We felt rather
uncomfortable.

He pays a visit to London Hospital:

We were taken over the students' quarters . . . then into the
dissecting room, and finally we were taken to see an
operation. Thank goodness it was only the arm being cut,
but it was all I could do to bear it and I had to keep saying to

myself 'he can't feel it' . . . It was the smell of the anaesthetic and the tremendous speed with which the operator worked that astounded me most . . . In the out-patients wards a large part of half a million people are attended to . . . I feel that every Jew should support the London Hospital considering what it does for the poor Jews of the East End.

The East End was not free from the 'white slave' traffic, as it came to be known, which was carried on in other parts of London, and Jewesses and Jews were to be found among the victims and the villains. The Jewish Association for the Protection of Girls and Women (planned and created by C. G. M.) joined in the efforts to stamp it out. Reginald Beddington (Sybil's husband) was a member and took Basil to a meeting which he had arranged at the Jews' Free School.

There were more than 200 girls of a mixed and varied type. Many were obviously on the streets at the present: as many, I was told, were reformed prostitutes. As many—and these were the really interesting ones—were on the brink of that awful abyss. Few of them could talk English, many had only just arrived from abroad. The possibilities of such a club struck me as enormous. But what it needs are West End Ladies of character and sympathy. Each one of these girls wanted help and advice . . . But the really desperate part was there were only two ladies going among the girls and talking to them, Miss Denhoff of the Sara Pyke House [a hostel for Jewish girls] and Mrs. Harrison, of the Association . . . Songs and music kept the girls amused; some of them broke down and sobbed . . . Oh bridge players of the West End where are you? How proud I felt of Reggie that night; I saw for the first time what he was really made of.

Throughout his pupillage Basil had made a reconnaissance in depth not only of the terrain in which he hoped to operate from his club but also of the views and experiences of the people, both East and West of Aldgate, whose support he would need. The result was a plan under which two synagogues, the West London at Upper Berkeley Street (Reform) and the synagogue of the Jewish Religious Union at Hill Street

(Liberal), should jointly provide the money and be the 'auspices' under which the Club should be carried on. By October 1913 the plan was gathering momentum. 'I went to the O.B.M. [the Oxford and Bermondsey Mission] . . . and visited G. T. who was too ill for me to stay more than a few minutes; then back to the O.B.M. and talked till long past midnight to get hints about the club and slept there . . . Heard that Hill Street [the Liberal Jewish Synagogue] had accepted the proposal to become connected with the club.' A few days later he is talking to a rabbi of the West London Synagogue: 'The idea was to persuade the Council of the West London to pass a resolution similar to Hill Street, that the club should be connected with the synagogue. The rabbi said it was too late: the scheme was excellent but he did not see how he could help. I left him determined that the proposition should at any rate be made to the Council next Sunday.'

Late that evening he extracts a promise from a friend on the Council that he will move the required resolution. 'I was hugely bucked by the many successes of the day; so much so that I determined to note the fact in this diary to warn myself that I am expecting a reaction when I shall feel pessimistic and despondent.' Then on 27 October, 'Heard that Berkeley Street had passed the following resolution: "That a grant of £50 be made for the current year for a boys' club to be started in St. George's in the East by Mr. B. L. Q. H." So the impossible has been achieved. I believe that C. G. M. had much to do with it.'

So far he had dealt with elders and wardens; it remained to win over the congregations. These audiences would have before them a man six feet three inches in height, fair haired, with strikingly handsome features expressive of kindness and humour, and, as he grew older, of authority. His voice was powerful and resonant, and he knew how to modulate it; later on, after a speech at Caxton Hall, a fellow-worker wrote to him, 'I have rarely been moved by such inspiring words . . . the light and shade of your delivery was a joy to hear.'

On 2 November he was to make a crucial speech to the Liberal Congregation.

Remained indoors most of the morning feeling perfectly miserable about my speech. When the awful time came we

28

arrived at the synagogue before it was open . . . I left mother
in the synagogue and returned to the vestry while the guests
arrived. Sybil and Reggie came up from Park Hatch on
purpose for it, which gave me all the encouragement in the
world. At last the beadle came in and told us that the hall was
practically full, and then we went out in procession and
Mattuck started his speech which lasted nearly a quarter of
an hour. I can't remember a single word said for I simply
couldn't listen to it.

At last it was my turn. It is stupid to boast in this diary but
for the 3/8 [¾?] hour during which I made my first speech
there was not a sound to be heard and the applause which
greeted me at the end made me think it had gone off well.

And so it had; congratulations were showered on him. Among
the audience were two Dockland friends and he took both boys
back to supper in Sussex Square. More than congratulations
came in; in a few days he writes, 'I have had to write nearly 20
letters every day this week. After the meeting itself we got
promised £130 and the total on my list is now £234.'

Finally he had to address the Liberal Jewish Association.

We set out for Miss Goldsmid's house in Portman Square,
where I had to make my old speech again about the club. The
room was perfectly packed with people and they all looked
so rich and smart and worldly that I was not a little nervous
until I got to my feet. The speech went down awfully well.
My dear C. G. M. was in the Chair. I used a phrase that I had
not used before: 'It is not Orthodox or Reform that we shall
be teaching, but Judaism pure and simple.' When I sat down
C. G. M. handed me a piece of paper on which was written
'Judaism that is neither Reform nor Orthodox and is yet
pure Judaism, does not exist except for you, but you are
likely to succeed just because you think it does.

You spoke admirably—so simply, unartificially and
earnestly; but don't say "awfully".'

It remained to make the premises habitable for the purposes
of a club and to hand them over to Basil. A few friends among
whom were a conveyancer and an architect formed themselves

into an informal sub-committee to negotiate with the owners, inspect the premises, and finally to convey them to the trustees of the Oxford and St George's Jewish Lads' Club, honorary secretary, B. L. Q. Henriques.

4

Birth of a Club

The first entry in the Club Minute Book is dated 3 March 1914.
Basil wrote to his mother:

> The Club is open! I had a terrible time the first day. No gas
> but a long row of candles . . . no games, as the ones ordered
> hadn't arrived; however, I was able to borrow some. At
> about 8 I opened the doors and let nearly 50 boys in.
> Imagine the muddle; semi-darkness, all those new faces,
> no-one with the least idea what the club is, me trying to take
> names, trying to keep order, trying everything at once . . .
> The boys, thank goodness, soon made themselves at home
> and we continued on until about 9.45. I started straight off
> with prayers on closing. They very seriously said the Shema[1]
> together and then I started an extemporary prayer. This
> made them roar with laughter! Most disconcerting, and I
> finished as quickly as I possibly could. Last night . . . I read a
> prayer from Singer's Prayer Book[2] which I thought they
> would know and the behaviour was perfect.

Two days later he wrote, 'The Club went beautifully last
night . . . The boys are most keen and very anxious to do all
they can to make it a success.'

At that time there was only one room for the Club to use. At
the top of the building there were two large attic rooms, one of
which Basil used as a 'bed-sitter' while in the other he
established a widow and her two children as house-keeper and
matron; her competence, hard work and native kindness may
well have saved the Club from perishing in its earliest infancy.
There was no bathroom so one had to make do with a geyser

31

and a cold shower. The other rooms, when they were ready for use, consisted of a 'canteen', a bare room furnished with two small tables and four chairs with a bar counter at one end; this led into a ping-pong room, which became a boxing room or synagogue at will. It housed three 6-foot benches. On the first floor was a 'library' without books and a billiard room with a 6-foot table. A workshop in the rear was used as a gymnasium; it contained a pair of parallel bars and the remains of what was once a vaulting horse.

The seasonal rise and fall in employment caused much poverty in St George's-in-the-East. Most of the workers were tailors, cabinet makers or bootmakers, and as mass-production increased work became scarcer. There was chronic overcrowding. Many of the children were undernourished, and both parents and children were often cold and ill-clad. There was one 'purpose-built' synagogue with a full-time beadle which stood out among numerous small Jewish conventicles, each of which retained the customs of that part of Europe from which it derived. The Club was surrounded, one might almost say besieged, by the trade and industry of the East End. It overlooked the cutting room of a tailor's factory and its immediate neighbours were a chemist, a pawn-broker's shop, a steam-bath establishment, a bakery, and a fried fish shop. Round the corner was Hessel Street Market, described by Rose as 'teeming with produce, customers, cats, chickens, dogs, children and dumps of garbage. Tenement houses and streets of tiny three-roomed houses, often inhabited by three families, jostled the Georgian and early Victorian grandeur of Cannon Street Road, at the end of which Hawksmoor's church of St. George-in-the-East dominated the dockland, fathering a number of small churches, missions and chapels throughout the area.' Her watercolour of the market is one of her best.

Basil was now free to apply the club-lore which he had acquired as a learner and to fashion his club after his own heart. He had begun by asking headmasters of local schools to send him eight boys, four 'good' and four 'troublesome', but not to tell him which was which. After they had joined he visited their parents so that he might better understand the children. Following the example of Victoria Club he soon introduced 'self-government' whereby 'officers' were elected, each to be specially responsible for a group of boys. Regular meetings of 'officers' were held which managers could attend but where the officers did most of the talking and were empowered to summon a wrong-doer before them and admonish him. The managers had their own meetings where they could discuss policy and finance. As is usual in boys' clubs the leader or whoever had ultimate responsibility had a residue of absolute power which Basil used, as may well be imagined, with great benevolence but on strictly doctrinal lines. There must be no heresy. On one occasion he closed the Club after a minor palace revolution. When he re-opened it he said to them:

> The Hon. Sec. must be a fellow who is in deep sympathy with the religious principles of the club and therefore X is not eligible. He possesses brains above the average, a great gift of the gab and a powerful personality. When these are found in a boy who is agnostic, anti-British and Bolshevik I doubt whether he should be retained in the club at all.

These or similar arrangements were common form in boys' clubs, but the nightly custom of praying together at the end of the evening after 'time' had been called was regarded by Basil as the essence of his method and at the heart of his spiritual teaching. It has been described, perhaps by R. L. H., as a 'deliberately invoked five-minute session of simple homily and dedication and prayer'. It was intended to give the boys the experience and then the habit of spontaneous prayer. Many of the members were to carry with them throughout their lives the memory of 'Time'.

As soon as the Club showed signs of being permanent a badge was designed. He got permission from the Oxford and Bermondsey Mission to adopt their motto 'Fratres' and the artist Horwitz designed the badge. Basil wanted it to be emblematic of his religion, his country and his university, so there was blue for Oxford, red for St George, Tudor roses for England and the 'Shield of David', the six-pointed star formed by the intersection of two triangles, for his religion. The whole was surmounted by the letters O.St.G. Great solemnity attended the 'giving of the badge'. Like other group emblems such as the scouts-troop badge or regimental crest it represented the unwritten code of ethics and behaviour on which the Club purported to be built and acceptance of it carried with it the responsibility of doing nothing to dishonour it. It was a great disgrace to have it taken away.

On 13 May 1914 the Chief Rabbi consecrated the Club. It was generous and broadminded of Dr Hertz to take part in a religious service with the Rev. Morris Joseph, the rabbi of a Reform Synagogue, and was a success so far as it went for Basil's experiment in catholic Judaism.

In fact each saw that the other could serve his purpose. In 1915 Basil had given the Chief Rabbi his reasons for saying that the English East End Jewry—he meant those born or brought up in this country—were becoming degraded and drifting permanently from their faith, while nothing was being done to prevent it. By 1919 the Chief Rabbi had become convinced that 'there was less need to "anglicise" the East End than to "Judaise" ' it because the religious sentiment had been lost. What they had in common was the hope that the return to religion lay through intensified welfare work based on the synagogue and led by a 'personality'. The Chief Rabbi, however, had said firmly that there must be no 'tampering' with religious convictions, and when he thought that those convictions were in danger the alliance came to an end.

It was a happy time for Basil. He was on the road that he wanted to take and would be content to follow for the rest of his life. The boys were his friends. A man who joined the Club in its early days and was for some forty years closer to Basil than any other Old Boy said that the distinguishing feature of O.St.G. was that each member of the Club felt that he was linked with Basil by a warm, perhaps even a loving, personal friendship.[3] He kept, however, to his original purpose of keeping open a bridge between East and West London. He joined the Reform Club. 'On Monday [he writes to his mother] Wood comes to the theatre with me. On Wednesday I dine with Lady McIver [C. G. M.'s sister] and on Friday Harold Christopherson dines quietly with me at home, these being my only nights off from the Club, so you see I am not losing touch with the West End.'

Outside the Club there was plenty of other work for him. He writes: 'I went to my first Norwood meeting . . . when my prayers that I might follow in my dear Father's footsteps were very fervent . . .' Before long he was invited to join the Jewish Board of Guardians (as the Jewish Welfare Board then was), the Juvenile Advisory Committee of Stepney and the Jewish Association for the Protection of Girls and Women. He was not born to be a committee-man *fainént*, and on all these bodies he worked hard, said what he thought and could at times be happily bellicose, so that at the age of twenty-four he had a practical experience of social work wider, probably, than most of his coevals.

When the war broke out in August the Club had to fight for its survival. For Basil as for many others there was the hard choice between conflicting duties. Of his brothers, Ronald, a regular officer, was killed, Julian was in the Queen's Westminsters and Harold, the eldest, was managing the family business. Above all, perhaps, there was the Club, with his sixty-eight 'children', to be kept in being. All the managers left to join the forces or to do war work. One of them, Leonard Stern, just down from Cambridge, was killed in May 1915. Basil writes: 'no one believed so thoroughly in the absolute necessity of a religious basis for the club . . . His place will never be wholly filled.'

Some of the managers would come back on their leave and perhaps spend a night at the Club so that it became a sort of staging-station for the Club's friends, who would 'book-in' for a night as they passed through London and sleep on mattresses on the floor wherever they could squeeze in and be happy talking to Basil of the past and the dubious future. He thought of these sojourns as the embryo of a settlement.

The diary of 1915 is the archetype of all his club diaries and set a pattern of club leadership which he never changed. He begins by tabulating the characters of each of his seventy-five boys, a line or two to each, like the headmaster's comment at the end of a school report. Thereafter the entries show him caring for each of them, probing their minds and motives, praising, rebuking, playing and praying with them but always as one friend to another. If occasionally the voice of the Senior Prefect is heard there was that in his character which could make them take it from him in good part. Yet the entries which stamp the Club with Basil's mark are the daily refrain that runs throughout the year that B. L. Q. H. or a manager or a visitor 'took prayers' at the end of the day, and with the prayers went a homily.

The 'activities' of the Club began to multiply, and he was glad to get people to run them. There was a gymnastics class, and athletics and swimming were taken seriously; they beat Victoria at cricket and were beaten by Norwood; Basil says the 'tone' on the field was good. Entries show that a Miss Bird came from Miss Montagu's club to take a drama class and a Miss Loewe took a first aid class, and that both courses were successful.

They had many visitors, both Christian and Jewish, among them his old friends of the Oxford and Bermondsey Mission, and his mother.

Camp occupies two closely written sheets; it was 'the most successful week in the whole history of the Club'.

In July Basil had said to Miss Loewe, 'It's no good producing good British Jews if you don't create good British Jewesses for them to marry. Will you create a girls' club?' She agreed, but said she must have a free hand to run it, and so, on 18 July an entry runs: 'The Oxford and St. George's Jewish Girls' Club was opened; it seemed to be in excellent spirits'; another runs: 'BLQH took prayers: subjects: camp; girls' club'.

5

Preacher into Soldier

In October 1915 Basil was gazetted into the 3rd Battalion East Kent Regiment (the Buffs) and was sent to Oxford for two months' training, with his mind, when not on his work, full of his Club and its members, 'his children'. By this time he seems to be not only treating Rose Loewe as his deputy but also considering her part in the future. She writes:

> I sent Basil daily long letters dealing with club affairs and individual boys, girls and workers; reports about the schools and how I spent the money he left with me for helping emergency cases . . . He sent me lists of people to whom to give messages . . . and long letters of advice on individual boys and social work problems . . . He questioned me on my view about continuing social work in St. George's after the war. He writes long expositions of Progressive Judaism comparing it with the orthodox tradition in which I had been brought up.

She included extracts from letters from Club members in the forces and the whole informal budget of Club news was called *Fratres*.[1] It was revived as part of Basil's war-work in 1940 (see p.101) and was finally made into a collection of letters, chosen from those which had passed between Basil and his 'children' at the front; it was published in 1950 (see p.155).

From Oxford he was sent to Dover. He writes:

> It was here I met George Macpherson, a boy of eighteen who had joined up straight from Winchester. We at once became friends. He had one of the simplest and profoundest faiths I

37

have ever come across. Never doubting his religion uplifted him so that he rose above the temptations which habitually worry fellows of that age . . .

One day George and I were sent for by the C.O. and told that we had been specially selected for an interview with Colonel Swinton at the War Office. There we learnt that a profoundly secret unit of the Machine-Gun Corps was being formed, but were given no hint as to its purpose.

Next day they were sent to Bisley. 'We had an informal lunch with Major Holford Walker who made the mystery more mysterious by telling us that we would have to "drive an armed caterpillar which would go through and over anything and knock down trees".'

From their training ground at Elvedon, Norfolk, he writes:

No firstborn child had ever been welcomed with quite so much excitement as we welcomed 'Mother', the first tank, and no mother has ever enjoyed playing with her child as we did with her. The training was one huge game and we used to look for trees to knock down . . . and would show off to the Brass Hats who came to look at us. One of the marvels of the war was the way in which the secrecy of this new arm was kept. No leave was stopped and no letter censored; we were simply warned, officers and men alike, not to make fools of ourselves and talk about what we were doing . . . Not a man broke this silently given word of honour.

'By the spring of 1916', writes R. L. H., 'Basil had decided that he could not visualise himself coping single-handed with St. George's after the war but that he and I together could forge ahead . . . The outcome was that we became engaged on 27 June, 1916.'

On 19 July 1916 Basil Henriques and Rose Loewe were married at St John's Wood Synagogue, London; Lance Huntingdon, the Resident at the Oxford and Bermondsey Mission was best man. After a family wedding breakfast at her parents' house they drove to Halls Green, Sevenoaks, so that Basil could say a prayer in the little chapel of the O.B.M., where he first experienced the happiness of social work.

Writing to his mother about their 'going away' taxi-ride he says:

> We went to C. G. M. for three minutes while the car went to get petrol. As Bunny[2] wanted to change we suddenly went to the Club in Cannon Street Road and there we had the most unique and wonderful tea with three of our boys and one of our girls who just took it all as a matter of course and were as natural and happy as you can imagine. St. George's had got to hear we were there and Cannon Street Road was crowded with people who cheered and yelled as we left on our way to Halls Green.

They found the chapel left empty for their private prayer; the Cross had been removed from the altar and an Old Testament put in its place.

Within a few days he was in France and by a happy chance Barclay Baron of the Oxford and Bermondsey Mission and Miss Hall, a supervisor at St George's Schools, were the first people he met at the British Officers' Club. Then, after a few days of final preparations such as training in the use of gas masks and care of carrier pigeons, they moved up to the front.

Bunny writes: 'The first battle in which he took part was on the Somme, in the area of Morval and Thiepval. I have collated the story from his Official Report, his description in his book *Indiscretions of a Warden*, his letters to me immediately after the battle and my own vivid recollections of the period when he was invalided back to London.'

> Our Section of three Tanks, including George's and mine, had Morval as the objective. Neither of us had the least idea what the Somme battle looked like; we had had no training with the Infantry, even at home, and the Infantry with whom we were to fight had never heard of us until they actually saw us in battle. We had never driven in England with our flaps closed, so that we had never used the periscope, and we had only driven with a clear view ahead on perfectly even ground.
>
> It must be remembered that the first Tanks had two huge wheels behind, which acted as rudders. They answered fairly

well on good ground, though it was terrifically hard work for the driver on the steering-wheel even then: but the trouble came when one wanted to turn sharply to the left or right. The back wheels then had to be raised, and the gears invariably jammed in the process, and the Tank then revolved on its own pivot. When the engine was going it was impossible to hear anything said to you from the outside. Guiding instructions were therefore given by hand signals; two or three people would always try to tell you what to do, waving their arms in both directions, one got more and more irritated, particularly as the heat increased inside.

With my six feet three inches, getting in and out was by no means easy, but once in the officer's seat, next to the driver, it was not uncomfortable. Mine was a female Tank, i.e., it was armed only with five machine guns; the male have two six pounder guns and three machine guns. There were four men on the guns, two on the gears, the driver and the officer.

Thus we were a team of eight in a very cramped space. When the flaps and the doors and the roof-hole were shut the heat became stifling. When the engine was full out, the smell and the heat were almost unbearable. Added to this was the exertion needed to make yourself heard either by voice or gesticulation to the rest of the crew. The fumes were intensified whilst firing.

(The action about to be described was an incident in the battle for the line of the river Ancre, a later stage of the operations which had begun on the Somme in July 1916. Between the Guards Division on the right wing of the Fourteenth Corps and their objective, the village of Morval, was a small nexus in the German trench system called the Quadrilateral, through which a disused railway line ran east and west. The three tanks of 'C' Company of the Heavy Branch of the Machine Gun Corps, as tanks were then called, were sent to the division to help in overcoming this obstacle.)

We moved off from our Camp behind the line at 5.00 p.m. on the 13th [13.9.16]. We went in a long procession and progress was slow from the beginning, as corners take time in manipulating. Some troops rushed to the side of our route and stood open-eyed, staring at us. Thousands swarmed round and the remarks were very humourous. We seemed to cheer people up as we went. You felt as though you were a showman in a circus, and had to answer questions galore. En route, I met an Officer of my old Regiment at Dover and also Neville Talbot, who is now a Colonel in the Chaplain's Brigade and a son of the Bishop of Winchester. He won the M.C. early in the War in trying to save his younger brother who was wounded. We passed Julian's Battalion and I looked out for anyone I knew, but failed, so asked the first Sergeant I saw if Julian had been in that Battalion. His reply was that he was his old Company Sergeant-Major! The most curious coincidence.

The Guards have been near us and there were two Oxford & Bermondsey Mission boys whom I could not find. We were having a long halt when I suddenly found myself face to face with them—Smutty Smith and Tom Dean. It was great. For three quarters of an hour we talked Bermondsey. Then at about 8 we got onto the main road. We covered one and a half miles in eight hours. To add to the joy it was pouring with rain. The number of trees I broke, and motor lorries I damaged, and ammunition wagons that got jammed was high. Here the remarks of passers-by were rather different. No language could be too strong—and I think they used their strongest. The traffic was jammed both ways for miles, and the Military Police and A.P.M. were getting frantic. However, at last we got off the main road and about 6.30 a.m. reached our point of assembly behind the Front Lines.

There was a hard day's work ahead and we started almost at once—cleaning, greasing and oiling etc. etc. All our orders were given us very clearly, and the co-operation between Infantry, Artillery and ourselves should have worked splendidly. But at 4 p.m. however, the orders were changed. The enemy were still holding a portion of trenches from which it was anticipated they would be driven out, and so three cars were now told to attack these trenches and then carry out the original scheme.

At 7.00 p.m. we left our place of assembly, feeling somewhat excited but quite calm. Archie, George and I were detailed for work and we started in procession in that order.

The three Tanks of my Section left soon after dark, mine being second and George's third. We had never reconnoitred the route, which was pointed out to us by guides. As far as I knew, we might just as well have been going back towards the Base, for we had not the least idea as to where the guide was taking us.

Neither George nor I had done any reconnaissance over the shell-pocked Somme battlefield. Maps meant nothing in such an area for there were no land marks. We did not even know where our own front-line was supposed to be. We were told that there was a railway line on our left and that we should follow this.

After about half an hour of very slow going a breathless runner arrived, stopped us, and obviously had important orders for us. He had, for we had forgotten the pigeon's food!

Another half hour and the leading Tank completely broke down with engine trouble, blocking our narrow way through what seemed to be a kind of ravine. It was a fearful task getting past in the car, but eventually we both managed to do this, and utterly exhausted, arrived at about midnight at what we were told by our guide was our destination, from which we were to move forward at Zero minus forty.

After 100 yards George stopped with engine trouble. This delayed us half an hour. Then we went for another 100 yards and he stopped again, this time for good. I minded this awfully, for George and I had become such devoted friends that we did not care what we did together. His serene nature and quiet sense of humour had meant much to me and I would have liked to have had him near for the greatest of all adventures. Thus Archie and I proceeded to carry on together. The further we advanced the more difficult became the track. There was a guide in front with lights showing the way, and we had to go awfully slowly, continually backing etc., to get out of the way of guns, ammunition etc. Down one very steep incline, something happened to Archie's tank. He came back and reported that he was out of action and that I must go on alone. I suppose mine is the first tank in history to have fired on the enemy.

I must own my heart was rather in my mouth, for I knew

the Germans were strongly holding that portion of the line. However, on we went, the path becoming more difficult at every yard. When we were out of the valley into what would at dawn be in full sight of the enemy, our guide was to leave us, and most of the way was marked out by tape. Before we reached the brow I got out, stopped the engine to allow it to cool down, and examined things generally. Archie himself had walked up with us, and to our horror we found that more than half our petrol had been swallowed up. It was midnight and I was due to start from that point where we were then at 3.00 a.m. Archie ran back and by really fine work succeeded in getting us about sixteen gallons by 2.30. In the meanwhile I had walked up to our front-line to have a look at the route. I came back rather doubtful! Then we waited. Some dozed, some ate. I drank the whole flask of whiskey neat. I got fresh orders to leave at 4.00 instead of 3.00. 4.00 arrived and we steamed ahead, squashing the Germans as we went. We couldn't steer properly and I kept on losing the tape. At 5.00 I was almost 400 yards behind our first line. I again stopped as we were rather too early. There was to be a barrage of artillery fire, through which a space was to be left for me to go. At 5.45 I reached another English trench. 'Are you our front-line?' I yelled. 'Yes' came the reply. 'Where are the Germans?' 'Straight ahead.' 'What time are you starting?' '6.20' shouted an Officer. 'Don't stop here or you'll draw fire onto my men.' 'I can't go on yet; I must wait for the Artillery Barrage.'

I had been given forty minutes to do the journey to the front-line. It took only twenty, and thus it is that I crossed our line twenty minutes too early. I don't know how near the enemy I actually was at Zero, but I think I must have been pretty well on our Artillery Barrage line, and it is a miracle that we did not get a direct hit from our own guns. I removed twenty yards and waited five minutes but the Barrage did not happen, so I decided to go forward.

As the dawn brightened, I spotted the railway line, and made for it. All the time I had had the front flaps open, for visibility was far too restricted if they were shut; but after a hail of machine gun fire, I closed them tightly for the first time.

'God help us, boys', I shouted, and we moved on. As we approached the Germans they let fire at us with might and main. At first no damage was done and we retaliated, killing about 20. Then the smash against my flap in front caused splinters to come in, and the blood to pour down my face. Another minute and my driver got the same. Then our prism glass broke to pieces; then another smash—and I think it must have been a bomb, right in my face. The next one wounded my driver so badly that he had to stop. By this time I could see nothing at all. All my prisms were broken, one a periscope, and it was impossible to look through the other. On turning round I saw my gunners lying on the floor. I couldn't make out why and yelled to them to fire. As the Infantry were now approaching and as it was impossible to guide the car, and as I now discovered that the sides weren't bullet proof, I decided that to save the Tank from being captured I had better withdraw. How we got back, I shall never understand. We dodged shells from the Artillery, and it was just a preserving hand which saved us. I fear I did not achieve my object. This is to be accounted for by the fact that—1. the Artillery Command did not put up the barrage; 2. breaking of all the prisms; 3. the non-bullet-proof sponsions; 4. the fact that one car was not enough to do what three were intended to do. My driver, self and servant were all scratched.

It was like Hell in a rough sea made of shell holes. The way we got over the ground was marvellous; every moment we were going to stick, but we didn't. The sight of thousands of our men dying and wounded was ghastly. I hate to think of it all.

Just as I was reporting to the Brigadier commanding the Infantry, I met George, who had got his Tank to go. He looked aghast at my blood-stained face, and then, with a smile, got into his Tank and went off to follow up the slowly advancing Infantry. It was the last I saw of him. I have never heard how his Tank fared. I only know he was a great hero off the field of battle and I am sure he must have been one on it.

My wounds looked worse than they were, and I had merely to have them washed and to be allowed to sleep and then to rejoin my Company. It was extraordinary how I got farther and farther away from the place I was really making for—my Company Commander's H.Q. A first aid station, then a hospital train, then a hospital at Rouen, then a hospital ship and finally an opthalmic hospital in London. At every stage I tried to be allowed back to my Tank; at each stage I became more and more haunted that I was fleeing from the battlefield as a coward. It seemed so absurd to be carried away like that, as in a torrential stream.

The nervous strain in this first battle of the Tanks for Officers and Crew alike was ghastly. Of my Company, One Officer went mad and shot his engine to make it go faster; another shot himself because he thought he had failed to do as well as he ought; two others, including myself had, what I suppose can be called, a nervous breakdown.

On 18 September Basil came home, preceded by a telegram 'Arriving Eye Hospital; love' and accompanied by Bunny, who had boarded the ambulance, pirate-fashion, outside Waterloo Station.

He had three splinter wounds (from the prisms) round the eyes and two on one leg; his eyes were uninjured. On his discharge from hospital he reported to Col. Swinton at the War Office.

I begged him to send me back to my tank unit that afternoon. He listened to my experiences and then told me about George . . . I found it awfully hard not to show him my feelings . . . He told me to go home and await orders . . . At last orders came and I was sent to Bovington Camp, Wool, where I discovered at what speed the original Tank Corps had grown since the early days of the H.S.M.G.C. My original crew were all expert mechanics . . . the men at Bovington know much less about the motor-engine and my new C.O. quickly realised that I should not be much good at teaching them. I was therefore made Reconnaissance Officer, a position which I held until the armistice. Although I saw or took part in every large battle until April 1918 I never actually drove a tank into action after the Somme.

He describes his new duties:

I had to keep the Battalion up to date with information
about the ground over which we would have to fight, which
meant teaching map-reading and the deciphering of
aeroplane photographs. I also acted as liaison officer which
meant attending divisional and Corps H.Q. conferences . . . I
also had to do a certain amount of lecturing.

He worked hard—though with his usual diffidence—on his
courses of instruction, and passed his tests well.

It's nearly one and I am not yet in bed! I have been trying to
paint a map and . . . you never saw anything so hideous . . . I
see 'incompetent' staring me in the face. I am so untidy and
inaccurate.

The Club boys and girls provided him with enormous mail.
He writes:

You will just have finished the Sabbath prayers and I
thought of you all and prayed with you. The few seconds of
prayer each night are the most glorious moments of the day.
It is so peaceful and still, and God is so very near, speaking
and comforting and helping. I can sympathise with the boys
in their 'don't care' attitude. It is so easy to let yourself go
and slide downwards without those few seconds of
communion. I know I should. One gets so tired of struggling
and fighting, and it is so often in vain. Life's meaning is never
very clear when you cannot give yourself to others, and the
temptation is to wonder why and what for.

3 March was the anniversary of the founding of the Club.

I cannot believe [he writes] that the club will have been
opened three years tomorrow. It has been a wonderful
period in my life and in the life of many others. When I look
back on the first night and see the grubby, disinterested
group of boys who stood round for Prayers, and then
compare them with what they are today, it makes one realise

46

the marvellous working of nature. I have never watched
people growing up before, having been the youngest at
home, and the whole thing has been a revelation to me.

Early in April he was sent to France on an instructional tour
of the front to complete his training as a reconnaissance officer.
He returned to France lighter in heart than he had left it by
reason of his having discovered from a perusal of his former
commanding officer's battle orders, that he had not started too
early on the day of the action at Thiepval, and thereby brought
down a barrage on our own troops, for which imagined mistake
he had bitterly reproached himself. The course included a short
visit to a quiet part of the line, and he describes the
devastations.

The only living thing for miles around, animal, bird, flower
or tree, was swarms of rats. Villages and woods alike are
unrecognisable and roads non-existent.
    I am so tired that I find it difficult to think of the names of
the individual boys and girls. I am becoming daily more
radical in my religious views . . . The essentials of life will
essentially be the essentials of religion, if you know what I
mean, and this war and fraternity under hardships are
teaching us what these essentials are. We have all been living
in a groove, looking at things through blinkers, carried along
as the fate of existence carries us. To get out of our sunken
road, to open our eyes and steer our own course are the
ideals we have now to strive for . . . Certainly at 125 [the
Club] we have the basis of the real things, but I don't like the
fringes we have to leave which collect the dust and the things
we don't want . . . If I don't get time to write to Mother will
you tell her I am itchy but well.

He rejoined his company in England on 23 April 1917 and
after embarkation leave his battalion was sent to the front. He
was present at the battles of Arras and Messines for instruction,
and fought in the battles of Ypres and Bapaume as Company
Reconnaissance Officer. After the battle of Ypres he writes (on
a piece of squared paper):

Just a line for goodnight; by Jove, it's Friday, or rather Saturday, so a good Sabbath to you. Read below as a love-letter: Very well, very tired, very keen, very wet . . . I wish I weren't quite so tired because I have many things to thank God for, but am certain that I shall fall asleep in the middle . . . The Brigadier says in his report:- 'The whole success is largely due to the excellent work done by the Reconnaissance Officer' . . . Can you guess how I loathe the sights and the noise and the ugliness and the futility of it all? . . . I am ¼ parson ¼ soldier ¼ good ¼ bad . . . I ought to answer some Club letters but I am too limp and tired . . . *Fratres* came today and it makes delightful reading, especially the news of all the others.

At the end of August Bunny again took the Club to camp at Halls Green. Basil writes: 'I have had the most beautiful letter from Halls Green, making me happier than I have been for months. It is like a wonderful refreshing drink, and I feel ever so much better after a fortnight of deep depression which has been scarcely possible to bear. It is magnificent that it has all been such a success.'

Towards the end of September came the Jewish Day of Atonement. Basil had intended going to the service held by the Jewish Chaplain who, however, fell ill, so that he spent the day alone. On the eve of the fast he writes:

I shall always think it is the most wonderful Holy Day of any religion. I intend fasting . . . I do hope I shall be alone tomorrow for I have a greater need than ever this year for a day of complete communion. I am not at all satisfied with myself and I need the new spirit which true prayer can and does give. It is not only things I want to get but things I want to get rid of . . . I feel very Jewish tonight and very home-sick, and now the vision of all the dear dead comes before me, and of Mother with her goodness and pain and sorrow, and then our dear Club children file before me and we are asking God to help us and show us the way ahead.

Much as he writes about the strain and stress of his work as Reconnaissance Officer he readily admitted that he was relatively lucky.

It literally sickens me [he writes] to think of the fellows up
the line tonight. It is really too ghastly for one's
imagination . . . Supposing you had walked six miles under
shell fire in pitch darkness, sinking above your knees every
step, carrying all your wordly belongings with you, and then
spent two days lying half buried in water and mud, bullets
pouring down on you and shells bursting all around, and
perhaps an attack at dawn, and rain coming down in torrents
all day and night and the wind numbing your fingers, and no
lights by night and no movement by day. You get a slight
idea. Pray for them, poor sons of mothers . . . Thank God
that it is not my lot.

Of his brother Julian, who was in the line with the Queen's
Westminsters, he writes: 'It is he who is to be pitied, not I.'
He described his part in the battle of Cambrai.

The battle was to start at 6.20 a.m. . . . and at 6.10 there was
perfect stillness, not a gun or a rifle to be heard. Then
suddenly at 6.20 there boomed forth a thousand guns and
more that had come up secretly . . . It dazzled and dazed
me . . . All one could say was 'poor old Fritz' and then
beneath one's breath 'God make thy presence felt with me
and make me strong and brave.' My job was to watch the
advance and then report . . . I strained my eyes to see the
tanks. At last I could distinguish their hulking forms
labouring up to the ridges, all in line, indomitable and
invincible monsters. At 7 o'clock I moved forward with the
second wave of infantry . . . I pushed on, bucked by the
exclamations of the Tommies who had won their first
objective: 'the Tanks did wonders' . . . At last we reached
our second objective; there there was to be a halt. We were
walking about in the open as if we had been in Aldershot . . .
I helped to re-organise the Company . . . I heard a voice say
'Hello, Henry old chap.' It was the Major [Major Fernie, O.C.
Company] . . . Night was coming on, and I had orders to go
back to where the tanks were to rally . . . We crowded into a
Bosch dug-out and I was soon asleep . . . We were up at 6,
and by 8 I was just behind our new front line . . . about 5
miles in front of what had been our line the previous

morning. Every one of our objectives had been gained.

So far Bunny's narrative.

In due course he was mentioned in despatches for his part in the action.

He got leave early in January 1918, and on his return to France wrote, 'The whole leave seems like a wonderful dream. Those nights at "125" are the happiest I ever spent and I never quite knew how much I loved the children.'

Enclosed in one of his letters were some prayers suitable for soldiers to use on active service. He says:

> It suddenly struck me that this book was really necessary. I wrote out a few subject headings and then went on writing all day long . . . It was not really difficult because they were all prayers that I have more or less said at sometime since I have been out here. I wonder if they are very poor and feeble; I shan't rest till I get your answer . . . Take them with a Fratres Prayer Book to C.G.M. and hear what he has to say.[3]

He showed it to the Jewish Chaplain, the Rev. Michael Adler, DSO, who thought much of it. 'I went to Adler's service which was very nice and homely and reverent. He does marvellous work out here and is an exceptionally able man.'

T.B. Strong, Dean of Christ Church and Vice-Chancellor, asked for a copy: they corresponded in terms of affectionate friendship. The link was Frank Haldinstein, a Christ Church man and Basil's friend. The Dean wrote: 'You have become very dear to me, first for F.H.'s sake, then for yours.'

Of the Special Order of the Day issued by the Corps Commander at the end of March 1918 he wrote:

> To go into battle with such an order ringing in your ears . . . means victory . . . Tell the boys to be proud of their country, to rejoice in the name of Englishman, to feel that no sacrifice they can make can be worthy of the great tradition of our history . . . worthy of the glorious name you bear—an English Jew.

Later on he says: 'I am rather anxious lest every pressure is not being used to get the boys to report the day they are 18, whether they have their calling-up papers or not.'

Next day he has news of one of his 'children'. 'Now isn't this letter from David Caminer wonderful! Lucky boy and still luckier girl! I am so, so pleased.'[4]

In April 1918 he wrote:

I have been in the thick of it, most exciting times and marvellous escapes. Got some sleep last night, the first for 4 nights . . . I will send F.P.Cs. [Field Post Cards] when I can, but don't expect them and don't worry if they don't come as I hope the worst is over; it could not have been much worse . . . I am perfectly safe and well, and back at our old Headquarters after a very trying and exciting week.

This refers to the fighting at the Lys Canal, and he described his part in it. He had been sent up with a detachment of machine guns under Major Norton to the support of an infantry division. 'I marched the men for a couple of miles into their posts. It was now dawning; we were told to hold a line about 1½ miles. I took the right and N. the left. The infantry had come up by this time and were digging themselves in.' The enemy attacked from the rear and Basil was ordered to report the situation to Divisional Headquarters.

After I had been there an hour a runner came back to say that Norton had been wounded, and soon after we heard that the enemy had broken through North of the Canal. Just at that moment General Elles (G.O.C. Tanks) [Brigadier General Hugh Elles] came up and asked what the situation was and having heard it . . . said he would go up and see for himself. He had his A.D.C. with him and took me along as well . . . We then got out of the car and pushed forward on foot. The General had not even his tin hat on, but his red and gold tabs. He was absolutely fearless, which was not my feelings at the time, I can assure you. He went out beyond the withdrawing infantry and choosing an exposed spot, sat down amid a torrent of machine gun bullets, took out his map and had a council of war. He then sent me back a couple of hundred yards and told me to stop every man on a certain cross-road, re-organise them and make them take up fresh positions. This I did and we thus re-established a line . . . The General took command . . . I was sent back to Headquarters to report and get some more ammunition . . . When I returned we were holding on all right . . . We were relieved about 7 p.m. by a new division.

Next month he was amongst those mentioned in despatches for his part in this fighting, and was awarded the Italian Silver Medal for Gallantry.

When Basil was not fighting, or preparing to fight, or suffering from overwork, or writing sermons, or compiling prayer-books, his lot was quite a happy one. His job as Battalion Reconnaissance Officer brought him into the company of fairly, and sometimes very, important people. He liked it, and pulled his own leg about it.

The Generals ask me to meals and we chat away like pals, and I do rather enjoy it. At the pow-wow there were six generals and eight 'brass hats' and two majors and your humble servant. I did try to look intelligent . . . Last night I had another painful ordeal as I was dining with a major-general and the Corps Commander was there to meet us. However, I really enjoyed it as the dinner was good and everybody was interesting. The day before I was with Prince Arthur of Connaught during the morning, had tea with a brigadier and then a second tea with a major-general, ending up at the Flying Squadron . . . It is interesting to meet a lot of new people.

There were other relaxations. His CO motored him to the sea for a few days' rest. 'I slept at Boulogne and in the morning I lay on the beach in a little fishing village and saw the white cliffs on the other side of the wonderfully clear blue sea . . . How I loved it and what a lot of good it did me.'

He met the Press. 'I had a most enjoyable time yesterday meeting all the war correspondents. They were extremely nice to me . . . Beach Thomas[5] is lunching with me here today.'

There was also food. 'The Major [Mayor?] gave me an

excellent champagne dinner, after which we went into their parlour and drank the most excellent brandy I have ever tasted.'

At the end of August 1918, when the allied victory was well on its way, Basil was transferred to England and stationed at Swanage, where he seems to have been employed in training reconnaissance officers, incidentally enlarging his own experience by going on a flying course.

After the armistice he tried hard, but failed, to get early demobilisation on account of his social work, and he was not discharged until June 1919.

Bunny writes:

And so, instead of groping his way up the stairs on account of sightless eyes, as he had envisaged and practised when he applied for a commission in 1915, Basil stormed, three steps at a time, up the three flights of stairs that led to his one-roomed home in Cannon Street Road.

He flung off his khaki and demanded his old tweed coat and grey flannel trousers, and sat down to peruse the Boys' Club Attendance Register. Thanks be to God.

6

Warden of a Settlement

Having perused the attendance registers Basil set off next morning in a hurry to get things done, and he continued to be in a hurry for the next thirty years. His diaries show the pace at which he lived. Here is a Saturday in 1923:

> Preached in the morning at West London Synagogue. Text Lev. XI 45 'Be ye holy'. Sermon went down well. Morris Joseph [the Rabbi] said my sermon was true Jewish mysticism and its success showed how at heart the Synagogue is spiritual. Saturday afternoon. Good congregation in Settlement Synagogue. Preached from 1 Kings III 9 'an understanding heart to judge the people.' Sermon went down well; an easy subject. In Boys' Club all the evening. Afterwards visited Old Victorians Club with F. and discussed East End Clubs holding dances in West End Hotels. Got back late to the remains of a House Captains' meeting.

In July 1927 he was lecturing at a summer school held by the National Council of Social Service. Here is his entry for the last two days:

> Lectured from 9.30 to 11 on 'Problems of the Adolescent aged 14 to 15½' dealing with after-care and unemployment. Lectured from 4.30 to 6 on 'Problems of the Adolescent from 15½ to 19' dealing with sex. Pringle [Vicar of St George's] gave a marvellous lecture in the evening on 'Shelley and Nelson' . . . Next day lectured on problems of the delinquent from 11.30 to 1.05 actually talking for 75 minutes. Caught 1.50 back and got to the Trocadero in time

for a conference on London Hospital matters dealing with visitors to the patients, and Jews in outlying wards. Settlement House Committee meeting at 7 p.m. Boys' Club (1914) Officers Meetings till nearly 11 p.m.

Finally a touch of the flamboyant. It was a Friday in April and he was returning from one of his American tours.

After a terrific race against time in glorious sunshine and a perfectly calm sea from Cherbourg instead of arriving at 5.30 at Southampton we did not get in until 6.40. Sydney Franklin[1] was there to meet me, Bunny having had to return to get to the Settlement for the Sabbath service. I wired that I hoped to get there by nine and preach. The train arrived at 8.55 and I rushed for a taxi, missing about 20 boys and managers who had come to meet me, and arrived at the Synagogue at 9.05 and preached on my experiences.

Generally speaking youth clubs in the early days were not to be classified as good or bad; they were mostly run by zealots who are unlikely to be lazy or incompetent. They varied, however, as they were rich or poor, and, more importantly, each might bear the distinctive mark of its founder and reflect his character.

In 1932 E.V. Lucas, the novelist and essayist who wrote so perceptively about London life, watched the boxing championships of the London Federation of Boys' Clubs at the Albert Hall. 'Having seen', he writes, 'the punishment administered with skill and vigour and received without a trace of lost temper . . . I wished to know more about the institutions where such a gallant spirit is fostered.' So he 'wandered' . . . first into the Webbe Club in Bethnal Green, 'named after A. J. Webbe the Middlesex cricketer, a friend of youth, and then to the Bernhard Baron Settlement in Stepney . . . In a short time I realised why the Albert Hall boxing had been so vigorous and straightforward . . .' The Webbe premises were poor, an adapted public house. 'The little chapel is an attic with very low beams . . . the boxing room has ropes only on three sides, the fourth side is the wall, padded but still the wall . . . However, the soul is the thing and the soul of the Webbe burns with a gleaming flame . . .' The Bernhard Baron Settlement, on the other hand, is large, purpose built (see pp.60-1) and has everything, but the same spirit is there. 'Never shall I forget those eager olive faces, those kindly eyes . . . I was delighted to note, although the billiard players were so immature, more than one honourable refusal to pot the white . . . The Warden is their big brother, stimulus, father and boon companion.

The mark which Basil put on his settlement is to be seen in the scope of its work; it was at once club, settlement and mission.

Club

At the heart of it was the Club, which eventually grew from the original one in Cannon Street Road into eight; three for boys and three for girls according to age, one for Old Boys and one for Old Girls. Basil was happiest when he was in the clubs; it was said that in the large rambling building in Berner Street (now Henriques Street) during club hours one could always tell Basil's whereabouts from the sound of laughter and Bunny's from the sound of music. Until he retired he never stopped being a club leader for all that he was also warden of a settlement, chairman of a juvenile court and by sheer hard work had come to be looked on as adviser on so many and various problems of social welfare. Few days did not end with an entry late at night such as

Old boys' Club meeting. Long talk with S. about Scouts (1923) or
Conference of managers of Boys' Clubs and Old Boys' Clubs Committees to discuss every aspect of the boys' side of the Settlement (1933) or
Discussion with Boys' Club Officers (1938) or
Spent most of the evening with X, an interesting case of embittered temper and jealousy caused by poverty.

The many meetings and conferences with the Old Boys which appear in the entries brought rich returns; in due course it was the Old Boys who, by and large, came to be the officers and to 'run' the Club.

The members were a fraternity and were his 'children' and it was in their clubs, in going about among them and getting to know them, as every 'Officer' does in every club, that he set himself to make a lasting bond of friendship between each one of them and himself.

In *Club Leadership To-day* Basil has set down what he thought a boys' club ought to be and do. Since he had collaborated with the three leaders of the boys' club movement in formulating for the National Association of Boys' Clubs their *Principles and Aims* it is reasonable to suppose that the paragraph cited derives from the joint wisdom and general practice of the Association, but the reference to religion is in his own style.

So too is the life of a boys' club. The sense of belonging is very real to every member. Each should feel that the honour of the club is in the hands of every member, and each should recognize the responsibility which rests upon him to enhance the happiness and the good name of the club. Once accepted as a full member, he should always feel that he is welcome in it and that his absence is a matter of concern to those who run it and to those who belong to it. He knows that in the club there is someone to whom he can confide his troubles and anxieties and who is fearfully keen about his progress, trying at all times understandingly to help him and to train his character so that he can overcome its weakness and develop all that is good in him. In the club he behaves absolutely naturally, unrestrained, except by the conduct required of him by the rest of the club. There can he relax and there does he meet his friends; he feels towards them a relationship akin to that of a brother, and if the club has a religious foundation, this brotherly kinship is a reality in that he and they know that as one family they worship and serve their Father in Heaven.

Some may prefer the simple and happy summary in his contribution to the Scottish Boys' Clubs Association: 'A Club should teach him through force of habit to play fairly, to think kindly and to enjoy naturally the beauty of life.'

How far his club fulfilled his purpose may be gauged from a few letters taken more or less at random from *Fratres* under the caption 'Club Spirit'. A few of them read as if their writers knew what was expected of them, but most of them ring true; the reader must judge for himself.

Every time I get in a sort of downcast mood and fed-up feeling I take my club badge out and remember what it was and stood for . . . The one reason why I am able to keep up the club spirit is that, while I was lucky enough to work at the settlement I used to see how the club members took the rough with the smooth and came up smiling. This made me resolve to do the same, whatever happens, and I hope to carry the same spirit through to the end. (The writer died after being released from a Japanese prison camp.)
or
I am boxing for the battery on Monday night in a bantam-weight competition and the Fratres badge will be pinned on the knee of my O.St.G shorts; I will be thinking of the club and the boys as if I were boxing for the club.
or
The club has helped each of us in our service jobs. Even in the short time that I have had a platoon I have seen, because I learnt the trick in Berner Street, that given a chance most men will do their best. (The writer was killed in action.)
or
The O.St.G must carry on because to all of us it is not just a building . . . a collection of halls and recreation rooms and gyms . . . it represents to us a way of living which we have learned to love through the years and for which we are fighting now.

An objective and professional assessment of O.St.G. is to be found in the *New Survey of London Life and Labour*, 1935, vol. IX, 'Adolescent Boys', where the Boys' Club together with

Repton and the Highway Clubs—'to mention only a few'—are described as being of the highest quality (p.175) and the Girls' Club (p.221) as an outstanding example.

Settlement

The clubs and the settlement were splendidly housed and equipped, but the gifts which provided these advantages were not mere windfalls. Basil had worked hard for them; the classlessness which he had originally planned for his cadre of club workers was bread upon the waters which returned to him by way of the right mixture of managers and administrators and fund-raising friends, [2] many of them from the sponsoring synagogues. He himself knew where money was, and he had a nice talent for explaining to its possessors why they should give some of it away and to whom. When in 1919 his club had outgrown 125 Cannon Street Road he begged and got the money to buy a disused many-roomed hostel in nearby Betts Street.[3] He had always secretly longed for a settlement, though he never expressly said so to his sponsors when he was asking for a club. Now it was within his reach and he put before the Home Office a scheme by which he was to have a Jewish centre in St George's 'and the whole of the workers are to be co-ordinated in the building which I am succeeding in getting the money to buy'. His many rooms cried out to be inhabited. In addition to the proliferation of clubs for boys and Old Boys, girls and Old Girls, 'activities' began one after another to find house-room within its walls, each answering to some local need. The Care Committees of the neighbouring schools (notably Fairclough Street, Christian Street, and Lower Chapman Street) set up their offices there while a luncheon club and a canteen enabled local social workers to meet and discuss their problems; there was a library and a musical society, a play centre and an infant welfare centre, and nearby a dental centre.

By the time Basil retired these were ultimately expanded in the Berner Street buildings to include a friendship club for the over-sixties, a luncheon club for OAPs, a Yiddish speaking society, a blind circle, a British Legion branch, a free legal advice centre, and (run by the synagogue) religion classes, and 'groups' for young and old, while the GLC organised a diabetes clinic, a treatment centre for minor ailments, and another for teeth. For the occasional return to nature one friend [4] gave them the use of land on the Sussex Downs for a permanent camping site, another [5] in 1950 a house in the Home Counties for use as a country club.

All these good works grew up bit by bit as Basil and Bunny could find helpers to run them and money to pay for them. There was a shortage of helpers. In 1909 a scheme for the sponsorship of East End districts by West End synagogues had been put forward by an orthodox rabbi (Dayan Feldman) followed ten years later by an almost identical one from Basil, yet although when he set about making his settlement in St George's 63 per cent of the school children were Jewish scarcely more than 25 per cent of the Care Committee workers and 22 per cent of the school managers came from the Jewish Community.[6] Basil and Bunny drew upon their sponsoring bodies, yet as time went on they came to rely on their Old Boys and Old Girls for club workers and, in the wider field of social work, on the allure of their settlement's growing reputation.

There was enough space to allow some of the rooms to be converted into a small synagogue which was duly consecrated.

On that day—18 January 1920—Basil entered in his diary:

A thoroughly successful day after heaps of preparation . . .
Prayers were read magnificently by C.G.M. and the rabbis
and the whole company was impressive, especially the choir
who were really excellent . . . there must have been 200-300
people present . . . The Mayor [Major C. Attlee] and I
spoke. He is an old Univ and Tank man. I was especially
pleased that Barclay Baron [of the Oxford and Bermondsey
Mission] and Eagar [of the NABC] came . . . This is the
greatest day I have so far experienced.

Ten years later when they wanted still more room, partly because they needed a larger synagogue, a friend put their needs to the philanthropist Bernhard Baron, who ultimately gave them £65,000 to buy the site of the disused Berner Street school and build thereon a settlement. It might have amounted to not more than £15,000 if Bunny had not managed to keep her nerve during a faintly melodramatic episode. It appeared that Mr Baron had begun by offering them £15,000 which, to everybody's consternation, Bunny refused. Some days later he came back with an offer of £65,000. It was a very great benefaction and rightly serves to link his name with the creation of the first Jewish settlement. It was opened in 1930 by HRH the Duke of Gloucester, as the Bernhard Baron St George's Jewish Settlement.

This was the second of the visits by which the Royal Family showed, as they had to many other clubs and settlements, their practical and continuing interest in service to youth and welfare. In 1927 the Prince of Wales had visited the club in Betts Street where he joined happily in the singing of Bunny's 'Camp Songs'; he came again in 1934 to open a block of modern flats which the trustees had built to accommodate some of those in the district who were most in need. A few years later the Duke of Kent visited the settlement in Berner Street and asked knowledgeably for information about everything he saw, and in 1949 HRH Princess Margaret honoured Basil with a visit to his court at Toynbee Hall and took luncheon with him and Bunny at the settlement. As President of the London Federation of Boys' Clubs and a Vice President of the National Association Basil was able to discuss cognate problems with the Patron of those two bodies, HRH the Duke of Edinburgh. He described these Royal occasions as 'a tremendous inspiration and encouragement' and the reaction of the club population shows that he was right.

The 125 rooms of the Berner Street building were designed and equipped both for the welfare work which had begun in Betts Street and for the pursuit and practice of all games and skills, arts and crafts which make for 'the physical, mental and moral fitness' which the National Association of Boys' Clubs declared to be 'the epitome of the teaching which all the activities of a club' must convey.

It was therefore not surprising that the club did well. Their boxing teams won trophies—Harry Mizler[7] had coached them—and so did all their athletes and games players, and in drama, music, literature and debate they were in the highest class. It is fair to say that Basil and Bunny who, like all good leaders, had kept a high standard in their clubs' affairs, were chiefly concerned that an O.St.G. competitor, if defeated, should be a good loser.

Basil would usually begin his day at 9 o'clock in a small room on the ground floor where he would 'advise' for two hours in much the same manner as a Citizens Advice Bureau. It was likely to be very good advice; he had worked for the Charity Organisation Society and he knew what, and how, relief was to be had. In fact, since the COS became the Family Welfare Association (which had an office in the settlement) and the FWA begat the Citizens Advice Bureau, Basil's morning sessions might be said to be the forerunner of the work of the Bureaux.

These entries, chosen from over the years, are typical and show how the Warden spent his day and the kinds of tasks which he was always accumulating.

1924
25 applicants in the morning. Went to London Hospital to have 1½ hrs talk with M about out-patients, L.C.C. children and nurses. Visited X [a club boy] in ophthalmic ward. Lower Chapman St. [School] managers meeting; was in chair. Extremely unpleasant meeting of Prison Visitation Committee . . . a beastly crisis has arisen . . . I refuse to resign. Milk inspection at Fairclough School.

1929
Prison. Visited young X. Children's Court. Discussion with Clarke Hall who is very enthusiastic about my suggestion for housing the Children's Court in the New Settlement. Very long interview at Norwood over Y who is suspected of crime.

1933
Funeral of Sir A.B. How dreadful to be so rich and to have only 40 people attend it and none to mourn you at your funeral!

1933 (October)
Went to R [a club boy] who has not had a good night. All
day at Appeals Sessions. Home Office Standing Committee.
I raised the point of under sixteens in Hospital. Evening
service (Friday); very full congregation.

1937
Visit from Dr. Stansfeld, founder of the O. & B.M.,
indirectly the inspiration of all I have ever done. He was
delighted with the Settlement. A great saint and genius in
religion.

1938
Prison. Addressed a meeting of Hostel Representatives at
Carpenters' Hall with a view to doing a survey and starting an
association. Boys' club. Old Boys' Club Special Committee.
Spanish Relief Appeal.[8]

There is an entry in 1939 saying 'visited schools all day with
Fairy [Hannah Hyam] to find a Head Teacher to recommend
for Christian Street School'. He had been doing this work ever
since Miss Hyam had first taught him how it should be done;
after twenty years the simple entry as part of the day's routine
seems to show how happily he accepted a way of life which
enabled him to play a part in all the work which was based on
the settlement.

Mission

While Basil's friendship was made with each individual member
he needed also to address them collectively, and the three
instruments of his message to his 'children' gathered together in
his club were 'Time', camp and the Synagogue. Writing on the
'Club Movement' in 1958, he said 'A Jewish club must infect its
members with Judaism. The club must be built up on the
"family" prayers at the end of the club evening. It is not
enough today that Jewish boys or girls are proud of their
heritage. They must live by their religion, understanding the
tremendous responsibilities of being the witnesses and chosen
servants of God.'

63

'Time'

'Time', the homily which followed the saying of a night prayer at closing time, had the merit of coming from the heart and sometimes, perhaps, arising out of thoughts or talks or happenings of the day. For Basil it had the utmost importance; it was a 'straight talk' tinged with the earnestness and humility of prayer. Bunny used to take 'Time' in the Girls' Club and on one occasion made a note in her diary, 'I went on too long.' The same commendable frankness is found occasionally in Basil's diaries.

'Time' seems never to have been written down, or there is no extant text, but we know what some of the club members thought of it.

One writes from the front (*Fratres*, pp.109, 112):

Twenty-two years ago I sat and listened to your first 'Time'. Something you then said has stuck in my mind ever since. Once you belong to the O.St.G and are really imbued with its spirit you belong to it for ever.

Another writes:

I still remember my handshake after prayers and the feeling of comfort of mind and security . . . when I first said goodnight on my first night of membership almost ten years ago.

These letters may or may not have come from the heart, but it is certain that the custom of 'Time' proved itself fit to survive in a community that had a keen eye for what was not sincere or genuine.

Camp

Basil left behind him a writing on Reform Club paper called 'Camp 1921' in which he says

God in all his grandeur is the great discovery that Camp has revealed, God unseen but felt—yes, but the same God, the same goodness and love which does exist in London exactly as He does here.

This was part of his mysticism; his reaction to beauty in nature was the religious experience of communion or the feeling of communion with its creator. On a fine night, when 'Time' was to be taken he would lead his flock up to the top of the hill on which the camp stood and talk to them under the stars in the belief that the beauty of the scene would make their consciousness more sensitive to the direct religious impact of his words. The Leonard Stern[9] sessions, prayer meetings combined with discussions on religion and morals—perhaps a sort of group therapy for minor spiritual ailments—were held in carefully chosen sites. He notes in his diary, 'A splendid L.S. last night on the south side of the hill looking toward the sea.' The effect was not lessened by the strange but picturesque garments which he kept for such occasions; a vast Tyrolean cloak and a broad-brimmed black hat such as one might bring back from a holiday in Mexico, while in his hand he held a formidable ashen staff, like a symbolic crook. Bunny unflinchingly mentions 'a pair of embroidered shorts' which, however, were prudently concealed beneath the cloak. All this was rather in the Basil manner. If he was to be the Good Shepherd or the flaming evangelist why not look the part? Anyway, it worked. A friend, one of his oldest Club members, said, 'I shall never forget the impression he made on me the first time I saw him standing there in the moonlight, his resonant voice rising and falling with the unmistakable sound of sincerity in every word.'

'Camp had been like living and seeing a new phase of life'; so wrote Frank Haldinstein, who came down from Christ Church, Oxford, to be one of the Club's first managers. He was killed in the First World War.

Basil was much concerned with the Jewishness of his camps.

The planning of the Sabbath in camp must be above all on the basis of its delectability. The family feast on a Friday evening in the dim light of the Sabbath candles on the white table; the quality and quantity of the food provided, [10] the glow that comes through saying the Sanctification . . . the peace, the love, the sense of brotherliness . . . The Friday evening fails completely and utterly in camp unless those who attend it have had deeply imprinted on their hearts that it is something good in itself, something to be emulated and repeated in their daily lives at home.

As to the secular part of camp he held the standard NABC views—which he had had a hand in formulating—as to the value of self-discipline, co-operation, perseverance, courage, good fellowship and so forth. In organisation, cleanliness and good order neither his camp nor Bunny's ever fell below high standards. That they were also a great happiness to the campers is attested by the yearly visit to Highdown when to this day, nearly sixty years after the first camp, Old Boys with their families spend a week under canvas to meet each other and remember their two club leaders.

Synagogue

As long ago as 1913 when Basil first asked the West London Synagogue to sponsor his club he said in his address to them: 'How can we justify ourselves in calling it a Jewish club without a Jewish religious influence? ... And why do we go to synagogue unless we draw from it support and consolation; encouragement and guidance from our communion with God at its services?' So he came to the East End determined to have a pulpit and preach his own brand of Judaism.

The synagogue can be said to have begun in 1915 when Bunny used to hold 'informal services' in the Boys' Club in Cannon Street Road, to which Basil used to come and preach when he could get leave from his regiment. She kept a diary for that year in which she noted the attendances, e.g. 'Saturday 7 August: 10 girls went to synagogue. XY came in late.' It seems that the boys held aloof for some months until shamed by the girls into joining. Thus for Saturday 28 August we read '15 to synagogue—11 boys—huge triumph for the Girls' Club.' On a Saturday in September Basil preached but Bunny for some reason could not be there. The entry runs: '17 went to synagogue. All absolutely enthusiastic about Basil's sermon. Oh, *how* I would have loved to be there.'

Then followed services in the small synagogue in Betts Street, but by 1919 the congregation was so large that services on the Holy Days had to be held in the Whitechapel Art Gallery. Basil on the eve of the first service wrote:

Spent the whole morning on the Art Gallery arranging chairs, and the Ark[11] which consisted of an oak cupboard on which was placed the curved back of the hall settee. This was draped in white silk damask. The Sepharim [scrolls] were placed in a covered box resting within the wardrobe. A fancy tin with a nightlight was set on top for the 'everlasting light'. For bells for the Sepharim we used silver-paper covered cardboard cones, hung with little silver spoons which tinkled as the scroll was moved and from a distance they made a very good substitute for the usual magnificent ornaments. The pointer was a silver meat skewer. There was a choir practice in the evening.

These improvisations look very much like Bunny's handiwork. She was generally but not infallibly an inspired improviser. The 'Choir Practice' is of the very marrow of this synagogue's being. Preaching forty years later Basil said, 'The choir was the mainstay of our services.' As soon as Bunny founded the Girls' Club she began to train a choir, which became the choir of the synagogue and in fact played a part in the development of the congregation and its liturgy more important than that usually assigned to choristers. Basil was constructing a reformed, or liberal, or progressive service in an orthodox or traditional environment, so Bunny, perhaps on the principle that the devil need not have all the best tunes (though she would not have put it like that), trained her choir to sing the traditional settings both for the hymns and the plain-song or 'cantillation'. These went straight to the heart of a congregation which had been brought up on them, and it may well be that without the choir and their tunes there would have been very few to hear Basil's message.

Basil has more to say about that first service, at which the rabbis and lay leaders of the two sponsoring synagogues were present; of the Second Day of the Jewish New Year he wrote:

Perhaps the greatest achievement in the whole of my life. The hall was packed full. About 750. Standing room only. Decorum almost perfect and with no books: choir splendid and the whole service moving and impressive . . . Indeed a day upon which to thank God for a realised dream.

Of the Day of Atonement he wrote:

A marvellous day. For Neïla [conclusion] service about
1000 present. For one and a half hours at the end decorum
perfect and tension almost unbearable. Pulverness [assistant
warden] reading most impressive. Sam read as well.
Preached three sermons during the day. One on sex and
gambling, one on Jonah and one on Peace. The choir was
excellent. I can't believe it all.

In due course a burial society was formed and then a religion
school. Basil severely pointed out that the society gave them
rights, the synagogue only obligations. He and Abraham
Pulverness, with invaluable help from some of the members,
shared the work of a lay ministry. In 1937 his assistant died and
a full-time minister was appointed, by which time the
congregation had generated its full complement of ladies guild,
men's society, and a youth group.

The Berner Street building was designed to have a small
'consecrated' synagogue and a large assembly hall in which an
organ was installed for use on Holy Days and special occasions.
This was the final and permanent synagogue and as long as Basil
was in London either he or his assistant warden or, latterly, the
minister preached or took the services throughout the year
until he retired.

He must have known how to talk to youth. When he was
about thirty Stephen Wise, one of the most eminent of Liberal
Jewish rabbis in America, wishing to have him over there as
visiting preacher told C.G.M., 'He would have a moving and
vivifying influence on such young men as he could reach . . . He
could get a hearing for our great spiritual message as perhaps no
other man could.' When he was nearly sixty he got a four-page
letter signed 'Archie Wavell'—it was the Field Marshal's
son—telling him 'How moved and stirred I was by your talk . . .
I called it poetry.' [12] Leo Baeck, the rabbi who had elected to
stay with his flock in the Theresienstadt concentration camp,
said of one of his sermons, 'That is the right way to talk to
young people.'

The entries in his diary show how preaching occupied or
even dominated his mind.

Friday, 22/VIII/1930. Took service and preached on
positive commands in the Torah. [13]
Friday, 10/XI/33, took the service. P. preached.
Friday 24/6/38. Took the service and preached on the
Sanctification.
Friday 3/III/39. Preached on Moses and the burning bush;
the sense of inability, God's promise of guidance, and
compared the burning bush with Bermondsey and with my
own continuous reliance until this minute on God's
guidance.

The list of such entries could be continued for nearly every
week during his years of service in the East End as warden of
the settlement. It is a record of his mission.

The services which he devised for his synagogue 'do not', he
tells us, 'correspond with any which are at present in existence';
they were a strange mixture of tradition and reform, with a
blood-transfusion of musical tradition which Bunny injected
by way of well known and much loved Jewish tunes. In some
cases there are paraphrases instead of translations, but the
Hebrew was retained 'in order to show the ancient thought
upon which the modern interpretation is based'. Besides the
ancient thought, Basil had to consider the impact on a Stepney
congregation of a Jewish service without Hebrew. His mark is
upon the service in the form of twenty 'special prayers'
composed by him each for some quality of character such as
purity, unselfishness, courage, sincerity, and, as has been cited,
understanding.

Of this prayer book the Rabbi of the West London
Synagogue said, 'The prayers come from the soul and are an
earnest endeavour to lead other souls upward.' The Rabbi of
the Liberal Synagogue said, 'I realise your difficulty . . . in the
almost idolatrous attachment to traditional forms prevalent in
a large section of Jewry . . . In your next prayer book I hope
you will be able to lead them a little further in the expression of
the ideas which you are teaching.' The Bishop of Stepney (Dr
Charles Curzon) to whom he sent a copy said, 'I shall keep it
not in my study but in my little chapel and whenever I use it I
shall be reminded of you and your work.'

The settlement is no more and the O.St.G. Clubs are

scattered and have local allegiances,[14] but some of the survivors and descendants of the religious community which first filled the Settlement Synagogue have kept the congregation in being in the East End. They have their own pastor, their own choir and they provide their own premises because the faith which once brought crowds to the Whitechapel Art Gallery and filled the big hall in Berner Street continues to live. It is the settlement congregation, embodying the spirit of Basil and Bunny and in its own peculiar way manifestly and admirably Jewish.

7

Magistrate

Basil has comparatively little to say in the diaries about his work on the Bench. There are perfunctory entries such as 'Went to appeal sessions where I sat until 4.15', or 'licensing justices', or just 'sessions'. Occasionally there is something of some slight personal or general interest. 'I waited for the case of H.C. when to my astonishment the licence was refused in spite of the fact that I insisted on an adjournment when it was to be put to the vote of the magistrates', or 'Had to decide on the interesting case of a firm that refused to pay rates to the Stepney Borough Council because they had turned off the light during the strike.[1] Our decision was that the rates should be paid under protest and an appeal made in the proper place.'

He had become a Justice of the Peace in 1924 when he was thirty-three. He was then warden of a settlement which he was doing his utmost to enlarge; honorary secretary and active leader of the Oxford and St George's Boys' Clubs and, with Bunny, ultimately responsible for the standards and behaviour of all the clubs which went under the title of O.St.G.; president and lay-minister of his synagogue at the settlement; chairman of a committee at Norwood Orphanage, and a Visiting Guardian at the Jewish Board of Guardians and on the House Committee of London Hospital. He was also a manager of three neighbouring schools. In none of these offices was he content to be and not to do; he worked—and often fought—as hard as he could on all of them.

By 1925 he was on the panel of juvenile court magistrates. An entry runs:

Interview with Alex Paterson and Mrs. Le Mesurier at the Home Office re a proposed scheme for Wandsworth. Alex thought that the Departmental Committee [for the treatment of offenders] would propose that there would be no short sentences for people under 21, but that either probation or Borstal should be the only two sentences . . . Borstal Institutions should be founded which would have the power to allow boys out on remission . . . Also that all under 18 should come under the children's court, which makes me particularly pleased that I have got on the rota.

He took on his new duties with his usual ardour and energy without giving any less of himself to his other work. He was lucky in having as his first chairman Sir William Clarke Hall, author of *Children's Courts*, whose knowledge and experience were largely drawn upon for the Children and Young Persons Act 1933. Basil, who said of him, 'He was a great master and taught me all I know', was elected Chairman in 1936 and sat at East London Juvenile Court till he retired in 1955. [2] He was chairman continuously for seventeen years.

Nobody had greater experience of his qualities as a magistrate or could judge them with greater understanding than his colleague ' 'cross the bridges', Mr John Watson, CBE, JP, Chairman of the South East London Juvenile Court, author of *The Child and the Magistrate*, or his Senior Probation Officer, Miss R. M. Braithwaite, each of whom has very kindly allowed an assessment of his qualities to be published here.

Mr Watson writes:

Basil was by nature a reformer. But as regards the juvenile courts he was a reformer within the existing framework; unlike, for instance, William Clarke Hall, who in an appendix to his book *Children's Courts*, went so far as to draft a reform Act which had an undoubted effect on subsequent legislation. But Basil was not a lawyer. Basically he was a social worker. His pre-eminence as a magistrate was his ability, when on the bench, to distinguish between the two. I am old enough to remember the days, before 1936, when the stipendiary magistrates presided in the Metropolitan Juvenile Courts. A criticism of some, not all of them, was that although they did their job conscientiously they were too much lawyers and too little sociologists—which was understandable, as that was how they had been trained. Conversely, I have since known lay magistrates who have allowed their 'welfare' interest to be paramount and to make them forget that more important than the immediate welfare of this child, or that child, are the interests and protection of the community 'without fear or favour, affection or ill-will'. I scarcely ever sat with Basil (we were opposite numbers on either side of the Thames) but from what I have been told, and from the attitude he adopted during our many, many discussions, he maintained an admirable balance. For that reason if for no other he was, I think, a superbly good lay magistrate, and not just a good one.

Miss Braithwaite was attached to his court as Probation Officer and became Senior Probation Officer in 1946, and saw him at work, and his effect on the offending children, on their parents, on witnesses and on all the officers of the court.
She writes:

Sir Basil was a big man in every sense of the word, his body, mind and spirit were totally committed to the love of God and the service of his fellow men. He was not afraid of his emotions and East London Juvenile Court would often rock with his response to the suffering or behaviour of those who appeared before him. He was well aware of the frailty of human nature but his belief in its capacity for goodness communicated itself to all those who came into contact with him. He gave of his best and thus demanded that others should do the same. Many to their surprise therefore found themselves striving to reach the standard of which he thought they were capable. Young offenders and officials alike would often quail before his cry of 'this is abominable!' when they had fallen short of this standard and then redouble their efforts to do better next time. Always young at heart and able to see life from a child's point of view, Sir Basil had a special gift for getting on to the same wavelength as the boys and girls who appeared before him. He could enable the most inarticulate among them to tell him their side of the story and had a bracing effect on those who had dissolved into tears. Above all, because he really cared about them, he gave them the feeling that they mattered. As one who appeared before him has put it: 'He made a terrific impression on me. I thought he was exceptionally kind, a wonderful man, considerate and most anxious to get at the truth. He looked concerned, he sounded concerned, and he gave me all the time I wanted, without pushing me, to explain why I had done what I had . . . He looked at me sternly, but there was kindness and feeling in his face . . . He did make a big effort for me and with me and I'll always be grateful for that. I look back on Basil Henriques with respect—quite frankly he's the only person in judicial authority that I've ever had any feelings whatsoever for, other than hatred and contempt.'[3]

Sir Basil was a great believer in the Probation system—he was at one time Chairman of our National Association—and an inspiring and beloved leader of the team at his court, never tiring of helping with particularly difficult cases, poking fun at the comic aspect so often present in the most tragic problems and thus lightening the load and restoring the sense of proportion of the harassed officer concerned.

Probation officers have lost a good friend and mourn his loss with the thousands of young delinquents in East London whom he helped in the course of his nineteen years as Chairman of the Bench. A young woman who had appeared before him seven or eight years ago wrote to him in Hospital shortly before his death to wish him a speedy recovery. She ended her letter thus: 'Well, Sir, I must close this letter now with my thoughts of you still in mind. As for me, Sir, I am trying to make good like you but I am certain you have made the grade.' Those who worked with him share her certainty.

Finally, a description in an article in *The Times* by a layman who had seen him in court: 'exquisitely tender but absolutely just.'

A reader of his diaries might add that he could keep his head in a crisis. In February 1927, he writes:

> Unfortunate predicament when I was proposed as chairman and somebody else proposed Mrs. X. I was temporarily in the chair. The voting was 3 for me, 2 for her. She then asked if she could vote for herself; I told her she could, which made the voting 3 all, with me in the chair having the casting vote. I refused to vote for myself or for her, whereupon she withdrew her nomination.

In the Magistrates' Association[4] he found plenty of work, congenial both for the causes which he could take up and the occasional opportunity for a broadside. He was very much in demand where knowledge, ideas, and hard work were needed. He became a friend of Margery Fry, to whom he sent a copy of *Fratres;* she called him 'exuberant and challenging'. Over the years his correspondence in and with the Association is a record of good work and shows, somewhat disjointedly, some of the ideas which preoccupied him. In due course he sat on their Council and on their Executive Committee; in addition he became a member of the London Juvenile Courts Consultative Committee and of a standing committee dealing with mental health. He was a member of a sub-committee appointed to draw up a report on juvenile delinquency; it was written in ten months and Basil left his mark on it by ensuring that funfairs came in for their share of the blame; a resolution to that effect was passed and sent to the Home Office. He looked upon gambling as an evil to be stamped out; he would have argued that it was a besetting weakness of the Jews among whom he worked and that he himself had had to deal with its calamitous results. Recent convictions (1975) of a vice-gang centred on a London funfair exemplify the dangers he feared.

Within the general field of juvenile delinquency his interest lay chiefly in approved schools and after-care, and consequently in helping the probation service by enhancing its status and responsibilities and improving the prospects of its members. To this end he and two other magistrates drew up detailed resolutions which were praised by the appropriate standing committee. When a memorandum on *After-Care from Approved Schools* was to be sent to the Home Office he made some observations on it. The Probation Officer, he said, should be the 'bridge between the home and the child'; boys should be licensed to hostels instead of going straight home from the approved school; 'the jump from the school to complete freedom is, for many boys, too great'. He staked everything on the character and personality of the Probation Officer. 'I do not believe it is sufficient inspiration to right living merely to give a child an ethical code. There must be a personal reformer for the child and for the home as well, and a short sharp punishment.'

He was touchy about probation. The Archbishop of York, Dr Cyril Garbett, was reported in the Press as saying 'probation encourages crime'. Without waiting to read the Diocesan leaflet in which the remark was supposed to be made he wrote a six page letter of protest. The Archbishop replied shortly and courteously enclosing the leaflet in which he had said, 'Probation, wise as it is, encourages crime among juveniles if given indiscriminately.' Basil himself had said that it was almost impossible to convince a child or his parents that he had not been 'let off' if he is put on probation on his first appearance in court.

In 1959 a conference at the highest level on the prevention of delinquency was held at the Home Office and Basil was among those invited to attend. He made the point that discipline was no less important than punishment and that the doctrine of 'no rewards, no punishments, no competition, no repression' had gone too far and was misguiding parents in the bringing up of their children. Fear of punishment should have a place in court. The Home Secretary (Mr R.A. Butler as he then was) called it a most useful contribution.

Prevention of crime, he said, should begin in childhood:

The thought uppermost in my mind is the number of insecure children from insecure homes whom I have before me in Court . . . I do most seriously suggest that the hours of work of mothers of children of school age should be regulated by their employers so that they can be home to greet their children after school and make them feel the

beauty of home life . . . I would like girls during their last
year at school to learn mothercraft, which is not the same as
housecraft, and to go into the infant schools and even into
the infant welfare centres and actually handle children and
to have instilled into them the patience and tenderness
which every mother needs to have.

In response to a request from a standing committee he
submitted a memorandum on approved schools. He drew
attention to the downward trend of 'successes' and considered
whether the fault lay with the teachers for not taking steps
earlier, or with the courts for being too ready to take a boy
away from his home, or with the parents for their neglect. In a
letter to a friend he said, 'I am somewhat perturbed that in my
own court I head the list by a long way for committing young
persons to approved schools, and yet I don't think that
Toynbee has a reputation for being harsh.' Should there be a
'closed house' for absconders where they could graduate to
open school when they became more stable? Was the after-care
at fault? Did the three upheavals caused by classifying centre,
remand home and, finally, the approved school so unsettle the
boys as to make training difficult? Should there be hostels as a
'bridge between school and home'?

He was asked to write an article on 'Absenteeism [from
school] and Delinquency', in which he accepted, after a careful
analysis of the facts, that the truant is a potential delinquent
and suggests heavier fines for parents who have not exercised
proper care. The paper was judged by his fellow craftsmen in
the Association to be 'sober and well balanced'.

Amid the statistics and fact-finding there was room for a
little pleasurable excitement. In one case he thought that a
clerical helper, whom they all knew, had not quite had her due,
or, as he would naturally put it, 'had been treated in a
disgraceful way', so he stirred things up, got together a private
meeting of the people who really counted and so moved her
employers that he was able to write to a colleague, 'I think Miss
X will get all she wants.'

The other offered a chance for a broadside. There was a cog
in the administrative machine, a competent and industrious
civil servant who had incurred Basil's displeasure. Of him he

wrote to a fellow magistrate:

> What a blundering ass XY is! I discovered that when I saw
> him in court. He always pretended to be so great and I found
> him extraordinarily bad. He absolutely makes me see red. A
> question ought to be asked in the House about after-care
> from approved schools . . . The insult of his lecture on
> approved schools and his smug complacency made me boil.

When he was on the warpath about child witnesses (see
pp. 109-12, below) an acquittal at London Sessions made him
boil. He often boiled.

8

The Day's Work

Basil would have said that he had been moved to live in the East End by a desire to save sinners, especially young sinners, to help the poor and to preach his gospel, purposes nowadays described as the prevention and cure of juvenile delinquency, redress for the under-privileged and the attempt to share with others a particular variety of religious experience. It was, however, not enough for him to be the full-time leader of a large boys' club, warden of a settlement, chairman of a juvenile court and the lay minister and general overseer of a synagogue. In the field of social service he had to be, like Teufelsdroeckh, a Professor of Things in General. So he worked away in what might reasonably have been his spare time at prison visiting, at spreading the boys' club movement throughout the country and in the service of the London Hospital, the Norwood Orphanage and the Jewish Board of Guardians, besides many less exigent causes. Some of these were perennial, like the Jewish Association for the Protection of Girls and Women, the British Diabetic Society (of which he was President) and the local branch of the British Legion; others were occasional, such as might arise when some hardship of working boys or girls, or (if they were poor) the sick and the old, was seen by him as a cause or matter in which he particularly could help. That is why he never went to bed before midnight and seldom before 1 or 2 a.m.

Prison Visiting

If Basil was a resounding success as a prison visitor it was because it afforded him just that sort of personal contact with the prisoners which gave him authority and leadership in his clubs. Here were souls to be saved, living animals ripe for spiritual vivisection.

At the end of 1923 he was asked to join the Visitation Committee of the United Synagogue as a lay visitor. The Chairman was Dr Charles Myers, CBE, FRS, the industrial psychologist. On 16 February 1924 he entered in his diary:

> My first visit to Wandsworth prison.[1] Got there at 11.45 and did not leave until 4.15. Interview with the Governor, Landers, whom I liked very much, and with 9 boys, 3 convicted and 6 on remand. I found it enthrallingly interesting. You seem to have the possibilities of getting a hold over the boys which can be got in no other place. Except for a villainously bumptious middle-class person in for a serious long term fraud who begged for a bible and a prayer book, and an ex-inmate of Colney Hatch,[2] all the rest seem to have fine possibilities. I was especially struck by the lying of a boy called X, who said he never had a father or a mother. Afterwards I was able to trace him as a brother of one of our nicest club boys. I fear that if it is to be properly done it will mean too much work and I may not be able to take it on.

The next three days carry respectively the entries:

> Wrote up prison reports. Did some prison visiting. Spent the morning at Wandsworth; 7 boys seen.

After that he settled down to his stride and as long as he was in London went visiting not less than once a week for the next 23 years. From time to time he found matters that required a remedy. In 1926 he told his chairman that he was worried because Jewish offenders tend to call themselves Church of England, the reason being that they have to spend Sunday in their cells instead of going to chapel, which is much nicer and instead of going to a concert of sacred music. Basil persuaded the Governor to let them go to the concert and they suggested a weekly educative talk.

In 1927 he was appointed by the Home Office to be a

member of the Visiting Committee for the Borstal Institution at Feltham. At that time the Institution at Portland was for comparatively 'hardened' criminals. Rochester and Feltham were for cases of 'normal' and 'mild' criminality respectively; of those who went to Feltham about one-third were mentally or physically inferior. In addition, however, all the Jewish cases were sent there straight from Wandsworth and ungraded. He was quick to perceive the consequences of having all the Jewish cases without discrimination in one institution. He wrote to his Chairman:

> Now it must be quite obvious to you that of the Jews a certain number of them would normally go into one of the other grades, and that the result is we are having rather a seriously bad type of boy, whose influence is not for the good of the institution as a whole, sent to Feltham simply because he is a Jew. As you may recollect there was a lad who I felt so strongly was too bad for Feltham that with special permission from the Prison Commissioners he was sent to Portland . . . But we should find it very difficult to arrange visitation for three institutions . . . I think it speaks most tremendously highly for all that you have done as chairman when I tell you that the Deputy Governor said that whereas a year ago the religious side of the Jewish boys was the worst run thing at Feltham he now considers it the best.

The Chairman went to Feltham and put the problem to the Governor. Basil approached the Prison Commissioners, represented in this case by his old friend Alex Paterson who of course did his best to help. Differences of opinion arose. Basil thought that if there were not enough visitors for everybody the 'hardened' cases at Portland should be visited rather than the 'mild' ones at Feltham. 'They are so very much out of touch with the world; they are more hardened and will stop there longer.' The Chairman (a psychologist) thought that the more hardened the delinquents the less likely that religious ministrations would have a lasting effect.

At length the difficulty was overcome. The Jewish cases were graded and some sent to Camp Hill (which took the place of Portland), others to Rochester and Feltham, and visitors were found (with Basil as talent-spotter) for all three places. The Chairman, not the man to give indiscriminate praise, disclaimed the credit for the improvement saying, 'it is all due to such ardent workers as you'.

The writing up of prison reports, which he noted in his diary the day after his first visit, was kept up throughout his service as visitor with exceptional care and industry. Dr Myers wrote, 'I have read your Wandsworth Prison Annual Report with great gratitude, interest and admiration . . . It is interesting and important to observe how clearly your conclusions in previous years are corroborated by the data obtained in 1928. Let me thank you warmly for all your help and devotion to this branch of prison visitation.'

Shortly afterwards the boys' prison was moved to Wormwood Scrubs and Alex Paterson on behalf of the Prison Commissioners sent him 'their warmest thanks for the patient and methodical way in which the Jewish boys at the boys' prison are dealt with by you and your colleagues'. He wrote again in 1936, after Basil had been visiting at Wormwood Scrubs for some years: 'Thank you very much for . . . your annual report. We do indeed appreciate all that you do for the Jewish boys who come to Wormwood Scrubs and only wish that for every 65 boys of Christian faith there was another separate B.L.Q. Henriques to attend to their needs.'

Before the boys' prison had moved to Wormwood Scrubs Basil had drafted some rough notes on the after-care at Wandsworth Boys' Prison. The gist of it was the establishment of a Discharged Prisoners Aid office in London under a whole-time officer, which would deal only with boys, both prisoners and those on remand. The officer would in effect be the agent of the DPA Society, and would exercise all the powers, financial and advisory, which after-care requires. Its purpose would be to ensure that 'no boy who goes through Wandsworth can return there without having really had a chance in life'.

The National Association of Boys' Clubs

In a speech broadcast in 1939 Basil said:

I have been travelling up and down the country a good deal trying to get the citizens of different towns and boroughs sufficiently keen—and I was going to say sensible—to put forward a really sincere and united effort to give to the working boys of their towns the chance in life which I believe is their absolute right.

In 1924 he had played a part in creating the Association and in framing its principles; writing in 1949 he said,

The origin of the association was a group of friends all trying to help each other to see more clearly what was needed for the boy and how best they could in their individual clubs supply that need.[3] I suggest that the purpose of the N.A.B.C. is the same today as it was twenty-five years ago. It is a fellowship of friends bound together by mutual trust; each in his own way trying to get a clearer vision of the kind of citizen we want to create and trying to learn from one another the best way of doing it.

He was its devoted servant. In due course he became a Vice-President and a Vice-Chairman, but his most valuable service was as Chairman of the Development Committee, which he became in 1934 and remained for twenty-five years. It was described by the Association when he died:[4]

From the springboard of his own club and the extensive experience which he gained he set off with all the fervour of a prophet to convert Britain to the cause. There can be few towns in which he did not speak at one time or another and right up until shortly before his death he was still drawing local audiences and holding their attention with the sincerity and power of his advocacy. At least twenty of the County Associations owe their origin directly to his personal efforts. Hundreds of clubs must have been founded as a result of his inspiration and passionate conviction.

A letter from a County Association whose inaugural meeting had been addressed by Basil shows why these talks can be called seminal:

Your speech was really one of the finest things I can remember. It lifted the whole meeting on to the highest level and showed us . . . where our duty lies for the future and what sort of standards we must work to. I don't think we shall forget the way you put to us the place and purpose of an Association. It was a grand and memorable night.

Here are some samples. From an address to the Lancaster Association:

Development today is not a matter of haphazardness but of organised development. It is the duty of this County Association so to arouse the corporations and councils of every city and town in the County to their civic responsibilities towards the next generation so that there is not a boy from these cities and towns who leaves the elementary schools without belonging to some voluntary organisation. We cannot wait until the boy gets into the police court before taking some kind of action in training him nor wait until the fine material . . . has had time to deteriorate. The boys of these two counties must be given the chance to grow into fit men . . . Institutional religion may be decaying but in its place there can grow up a new friendship no less sacred and holy in the fellowship of the club; a fellowship which can only be made real through the acknowledgement of a divine Fatherhood . . . What really matters is the individual boy—to know him, to understand him and to trust him. There can be no mass production in developing the boy's finest faculties.

From an address given at Portsmouth Guildhall:

Do you consider the working boy of fourteen to eighteen worthwhile? If you do, and feel it as I feel it, then you will realise that there is nothing that can be too good to offer him so that he can have his chance in life. I would go further . . . it is his right, for dare we say that there is one human being who is more precious in the eyes of his creator than another? . . . I believe that the citizens of this great city can form a splendid team to carry out this great work. You have such associations as Toc H, Rotary and the City Council. This Council can help much by offering the facilities of their swimming baths, of their laundry, of their public library, and even in the use of rooms. The old boys of your schools and the naval and military officers who have leisure time to spare, all of them can join together to work for the youth of this great city.

By affiliating your clubs to the N.A.B.C. you are joining a great fellowship of youth and men, which without any show of uniform or outward display is striving with heart and soul and might to create the glorious fellowship of mankind.

In order to indoctrinate the young he went to schools and universities to persuade his hearers that they had a duty to the under-privileged which could properly be fulfilled by helping to create or manage a working boys' club or in some way befriend its members.

This example is taken from an address at Stonyhurst; he delivered a similar message at other schools, among them Harrow, Stowe, Westminster, Aldenham and Winchester.

Unless Stonyhurst has given you self-assurance, culture, leadership and reliability it has been of little use to you.

Bearing in mind the contrast in upbringing it may at first be difficult to find a point of contact with the working boy in the club. If only you took part with the boys in the life of the club, boxed with them, ran with them, played football with them and above all went to camp with them then you have a common interest and you find there is extraordinarily little difference to choose between you.

You can only do this, however, if you are prepared to share in the whole life of the club without a tinge of patronage or condescension.

The future of England depends far more on the 850,000 working boys between 14 and 18 than it does on the 100,000 privileged boys . . . We would seek to form in England a great national team where boys of all classes and conditions are bound together by mutual sympathy and loyalty, born of the fact that they each realise that they are equally precious to, and are the children of, the divine Father.

Of course, there were the usual quarrels and reconciliations. The Education Act, 1944, had laid upon local authorities the duty of maintaining a 'service of youth'; clubs and other organisations with a mixed membership of boys and girls sometimes called 'Youth Centres' were springing up under municipal sponsorship. Basil was obsessively opposed to mixed clubs. How, he asked, could a mixed club be affiliated to an association either of boys' clubs or of girls' clubs? It would be a betrayal of trust if the boys in mixed clubs were suffered to be deprived of the saving grace of the NABC's tutelage and tradition; and so on.

The policy of the NABC was very rightly to ensure the survival of the unmixed boys' clubs; that was its paramount interest, but they were not, in principle, opposed to mixed clubs. Basil did not present his case very well; he did not support his prognostications by any evidence from co-educational schools and other such mixed youth groups either at home or abroad. Moreover he did not read the signs of the times to which Mr Punch had called his attention when women began to make shells and drive ploughs:

> Common are to either sex
> Artifex and opifex.

There were furious rumblings and threats to resign but events took a common-sense course. Where there is a clearly identifiable boys' component of a mixed club that component affiliates to the NABC whose clubs, by virtue of an informal concordat, happily co-exist with those sponsored by the local authority.

There were clubs which had run into difficulties and had to be salvaged and good men who had to be steered into jobs for which they were badly needed. Basil's position in the NABC and the LFBC (where he succeeded Field-Marshal Sir Claud Auchinleck as President) and his panoramic knowledge of the boys' club world marked him out as the consultant in any such case, and he was glad to be asked to help.

Some time in 1945 Basil had been present at the opening of the Britannia Club in Hoxton. In 1946 a letter from the Chairman told him that their hopes of going ahead and

Plate 2(a) Basil, aged six, page to the Lady Mayoress at a Mansion House reception, 1896

Plate 2(b) Basil, aged fourteen, about the time he entered Harrow, 1904

Plate 3 Freshman at University College, Oxford, 1910

Plate 4 Wedding of Basil and Rose Loewe at St John's Wood Synagogue,
London, 19 July 1916

Plate 5   The camp on Highdown Hill near Steyning
on the site lent by Sir Frederic Stern, about 1926

Plate 6(a) The club leader with his 'children'

Plate 6(b) The Bernhard Baron St George's Jewish Settlement, built in 1930, drawn by Enid Dreyfus

Plate 7 In the film *Children on Trial*; the figure on the right is not a 'delinquent' but is acting the part

Plate 8 CBE; leaving the Palace after the investiture, 1948

becoming useful and valued had been disappointed; diligent but ineffective leadership and lack of money had been the main causes, and the club would have to close. What could be done? Basil replied that he well remembered the club and knew something about it; it suffered from weak leadership. He advised them to ask the Training Secretary of the NABC to recommend them a really strong leader, and told them he would do his utmost to help the club which was badly needed in that district. The Chairman wrote, 'Your letter has changed the whole outlook of the committee . . . We are going to try to carry on and if we can get new leadership we have a chance to do some useful work, and will do all we can to make the Boys' Club flourish.' At the same time Basil wrote to the local superintendent of police asking their help on the ground that a good boys' club in Hoxton meant less work for them. They were glad to co-operate and agreed to send young police officers to act as club leaders. And so the club was saved.

The Lion Boys' Club, also in Hoxton, were told that the building which they occupied (apparently as tenants at sufferance) was to be put on the commercial market. The London Federation of Boys' Clubs wrote a report on it which found its way, presumably not by accident, into Basil's hands. The President of the LFBC wrote to him.

> Dear Basil, I am very glad to hear from the Development Secretary that you were prepared to go on the warpath about the Lion Boys' Club.

Basil went into action with a letter to the Federation:

> Writing as Chairman of the East London Juvenile Court I want to say that this [the closing of the club] would be an absolute tragedy. Hoxton is one of the districts in which there is a great deal of juvenile delinquency and the Lion Club has done such excellent work in taking in potential delinquents and turning them into honest fellows . . . If Hoxton is to lose a club which is doing such extremely valuable work as the Lion Boys' Club I am convinced there would be a serious rise in juvenile delinquency in that area.

The club asked, 'May we quote your letter? . . . Coming from you it should be an immense help in backing an appeal.' To which Basil answered, 'That is why I wrote it.' The appeal was made, money came in, and the club was saved.

The letter is interesting for another reason. It was not his practice to make membership of a club a condition of probation, but he did try to get boys who had been through his court to join one voluntarily. He had, however, been rebuffed (so he said) by clubs which did not want members whose 'delinquency' might spoil the club, and so he wrote to the Chairman of the NABC:

I felt that I have so often emphasised that *today* clubs do not exist to keep boys off the streets and do not have as their main purpose the prevention of delinquency that we have let the pendulum swing too far, and now clubs are afraid of 'taking in' the worst boys lest such boys should spoil the tone of the club. The time has now come for the pendulum to swing in the other direction, and for clubs once more to say that their primary object is to take in the worst boys, 'delinquent' or not, and try to turn them into decent citizens, rather than to give 'further education' to boys who are now getting further education in grammar schools. Believing as I do that clubs can save 'sinners' and also having been influenced by you and my other Christian friends to be particularly perturbed about the few lost sheep I feel that clubs must once more seek out the lost sheep and have an ever open door to welcome back the prodigal sons. The rest of the flock may not grow up as noble as they should have been had they been properly shepherded, but on the whole they are not likely to go badly wrong without the club whereas the weak in mind and spirit are likely to become utterly lost unless places like clubs are prepared to set out, as indeed clubs did when they first started, to help them . . . A really good club can often do for a probationer as much as an approved school.

X, who had been a Senior Boys' Training Officer to the NABC was minded to emigrate. He wrote to Basil asking for information about opportunities awaiting club leaders in

Australia which Basil had stressed in an NABC conference at Edinburgh. Basil wrote, 'I am interested to hear that you are thinking of the Dominions. I do know that Victoria is frantically in need of a Training Officer for the Victoria Association of Boys' Clubs. You would be the ideal person for this and I do not think it would be too difficult to arrange for you to go over there for that purpose . . . If you would like this post I could put you on to the right people to invite you.' Then, to the boys' club in Victoria: 'My dear K, I believe I have got hold of the ideal fellow for you in Captain X . . . I have told him to write to you.'

The London Hospital

When Basil established his club in 1914 National Health Insurance was only three years old. A wage-earner who had contributed fourpence a week towards his insurance would be entitled to ten shillings a week while he was sick and to free medicine and treatment from a 'panel' doctor, but apart from a maternity benefit of thirty shillings none of his dependants received any benefit under the scheme. After the war the scale of payment was increased to conform to the rising cost of living, but still no provision was made for the wage-earner's family. The scheme did not cover hospital treatment, for which the people in Basil's district had to rely on the London Hospital and the two Poor Law infirmaries now called St George's Hospital and St Peter's Hospital.[5] The London was some eighty beds short of its waiting list.

In *Indiscretions of a Warden* Basil tells how he came to be on the House Committee of the London. One night in 1920 he was called to the home of a discharged soldier who was dying in circumstances of the utmost poverty and squalor. He tried to get a nurse from the private staff of the London to sit with him for the night but was refused. He wrote a very rude letter to the chairman of the hospital, Lord Knutsford,[6] who sent for him and by way of rebuke read to him their rules about their private nursing staff. Then he said, 'You don't seem half such a beastly fellow as your letters would make you out to be. Why don't you come and help us and join the House Committee?' So he joined their Committee and worried them for the next twenty years, because he was incapable of leaving ill alone. Yet the hospital was glad to be worried. A House Governor writes, 'I will go carefully into the cases you mention . . . Please do not apologise for worrying.' Lord Knutsford (he always signed himself K when writing to his friends), answering one of his complaints about the treatment of an out-patient, says, 'You are really, please, not to write to me as if I was a good boy for having taken pains to get to the bottom of complaints. It is my job and yours and we both want the London Hospital spirit to be active everywhere.' Most of his complaints were about the treatment of out-patients, because he was spending his life among the people from whom the out-patients came; perhaps it was an advantage to the hospital to have the cases put forward by one who knew the necessities and the temperament of the out-patients as well as the workings of the hospital and the difficulties which beset it. There had, of course, always been difficulties with the Out-Patients Department, as in most hospitals. In 1924, the Out-Patients Committee, reporting on the subject to the House Committee, saw the root cause of it in the lack of parity of esteem with the In-Patients Department.

The particular complaint about which the Chairman wrote concerned payment of the hospital fee. The London, like all the other hospitals which were supported entirely by voluntary contributions, was always short of money and the payment of a fee meant much to it. In 1913 there were about 175,000 out-patients, of whom only some 20,000 were insured; about 35 per cent of those treated were found by the enquiry officers to be unable to pay anything and were therefore treated free. The income from annual subscription was about £13,850; all the rest had to come from the King's Fund, the Hospital Sunday Fund, the 'Voucher Societies', legacies, donations and collecting boxes. In 1921, the hospital, with a total income of £253,474, was passing through what K called a terrible financial crisis. K had asked Basil to launch an appeal to the Jewish community in view of the number of Jews treated—about 2,000 in-patients and 24,000 out-patients—and the special facilities accorded to them. To that end Basil had addressed a great meeting at what was then the People's Palace and is now Queen Mary College. The Rev. J. F. Stern, father of his friend,

Leonard Stern, wrote to him next day, 'It was a big thing and a great thing ... and you alone, dear chap, in all East London could have accomplished it ... Lord K was looking on with wonder ... gratification and gratitude.' It is against that background that Basil's complaints and the rules of the hospital must be regarded. The rule was that each patient, if he could afford it, had to pay a shilling for each visit, which covered registration and one week's supply of medicine and dressings. If they had not got the shilling they might be sent home to get it. The enquiry officer decided who could pay.

On this occasion a mother brought her sick child; she had not got the shilling but the enquiry officer, being satisfied, told her that she might bring it on her next visit. An enquiry officer in another department to which she had been sent, not knowing of the former order, said that until the shilling was paid she could not have the medicine. Clearly a human error, and as such frankly acknowledged by the House Governor, but in writing about it to the Chairman, Basil had referred to it as one among 'continuous troubles'. The Chairman writes back, 'These are not, my dear Basil H, continuous troubles. They do arise now and again but considering the number of people, poor, ignorant, all out for their rights, all out against officials, some seeking offence where none is meant, I do not think we can speak or think of the complaints as continuous.' Basil had also written:

> I should like to suggest to P, if you approve, that we give orders that a patient is to be trusted to bring the shilling next time, and is *never* sent home to fetch it ... Why shouldn't we trust people to fulfil a promise? The average man does not wilfully want to do the hospital down. He may like to get a thing on the cheap, but I don't believe he wants to cheat the hospital. I have found in dealing with people round here that they do so very much more when they feel they are trusted. Their honour is at stake and except for Chairmen of Hospitals, and other beggars,[7] the average man is proud of his honour.
>
> Quite apart from all this, don't you think that a person must be jolly poor who does not walk about with at least a shilling in his pocket?

To which K answers: 'I agree about the sending home to get the shilling . . . I think you and P. might suggest a relaxation of the rule. But on the other hand, you heard what D. said that he had found that many people never did send the money if allowed to go without paying, and of course now that we give so much more for the flat rate of a shilling it is important to get that shilling.' It was the argument of maturity against ardour.

The matters which moved Basil to intervene do not seem very weighty in relation to the purposes and problems of a great teaching hospital, but they touched the out-patients in a way that he, their friend and niehgbour, could vividly understand. There was the question of the hours at which out-patients could be seen, which might often be such as to prevent a wage-earner from attending without loss of earnings; the time a patient might have to wait for admittance, which might be short if he could afford to be seen and recommended by a specialist; the charge made by the LCC for taking a 'stretcher case' by ambulance, ten shillings plus a waiting fee; he calls it 'a cruelly unnecessary expense'; and finally the return home of children after tonsillectomy without a period of recuperation in hospital.

Most of these matters had come before one or more or all of the committees of the hospital to be investigated and worked upon over the years, but remedies had to wait upon resources; good will was not always enough. When Basil said[8] that he did not feel as if he had been of the slightest use to the hospital he did himself less than justice. It would be truer to say that he became one of a band of enthusiasts working for a common purpose, who welcomed him both as a critic and a friend, and who gave him full credit for a share in their achievements. K used to speak of him as 'that good fellow Henriques'.

The Jewish Orphanage, Norwood, and the Jewish Board of Guardians

In these great charities Basil was working for boys both individually and collectively. He was a committee-man at Norwood for 46 years and with the Board (now the Jewish Welfare Board) for 37, quarrelling with each of them from time to time but always their untiring servant.

In respect of care—indeed, loving care—for the body, mind and soul of each of its children (not all orphans) the Jewish Orphanage at Norwood since its foundation in 1795 had been a first-rate institution. But it was none the less an institution and the post-Victorian tendency was so to modify the tutelage that the care remained while the institution withered away. The Curtis report (1946 Cmd 6922) recommended that in all cases foster homes were to be preferred where possible to hostels, and the change is marked in the new name: 'The Norwood Homes for Jewish Children', and in its new function 'to provide residential homes for children and young people in need of care and to make provision for their after-care'. In the House Committee the traditionalists were firmly entrenched and Basil was tactfully not invited to chair it, but he was Chairman of the After-Care (Boys) Committee, with nothing to stop him from leading his committee in a movement to implement the new doctrine.

He had been invited to join Norwood in 1914. He writes: 'I went to my first Norwood meeting . . . There was such a general cry that I should be on the House Committee as well as the Apprenticing Committee that I finally agreed.' He had joined the Army in 1915 and was not back again managing his club until 1919; by that time he can scarcely have acquired enough experience of the working of Norwood to justify him in giving its committees a good talking-to. That, however, is just what he did. Without any of the inhibitions of a newcomer he sends to the Employment Committee a five-page report, written from the Reform Club.

It is a far-reaching and comprehensive and very competent document intended 'to lay down a thorough and systematic basis' on which after-care should proceed. A system of guardians (which had once existed) is to be re-introduced, such guardians being preferably managers of clubs or 'young men of the community', each to have under his care one or two of the boys 'to whom he is to be a special friend'. He lays down in great detail the duties of the guardians as well as those of a new secretary who is to be appointed to do the work of registrar of after-care. Two suggestions are characteristic: 'a regular system of moral education' should be provided for boys of twelve years and upwards, while an Old Boys' Association should be formed for boys between fourteen and eighteen; 'subscriptions should be enforced from all members and nothing in the way of treating should be encouraged'. That is how it was done at O.St.G.

It must be observed that the subscribers to Norwood were very largely traditionally minded Jews who regarded the up-bringing of the Norwood children as something of a religious duty, and in regard to such duties traditional Jews are not generally over-zealous in the pursuit of change. After all, the children were well fed, well clothed, well taught and well grounded in their religion, and, above all, happy. What need, therefore, for these new-fangled notions? In such circumstances a little complacency was perhaps to be expected.

Basil had a way of jumping on a bandwagon and then taking over the reins, which could cause difficulties, and perhaps an upset. The difficulties here were for the Chairman of Norwood, then Anthony de Rothschild, Basil's good friend, but having the responsibility of ensuring the flow of money from the many charitable traditionalists and thereby the viability of Norwood. He knew that change was only a question of time, but Basil would keep whipping up the horses; one day he arrived there with two hundred flannel shirts, soft collars and ties for the boys to wear instead of their institutional dress. Later there is an entry: 'The Chairman of the House Committee turned down nearly the whole of G's recommendations which were really my recommendations under G's name.' Then again: 'attended a general meeting where the G report came up; every suggestion turned down. I made a very fatuous and stupid speech on the whole system of Norwood.' In due course he sends in his resignation, but withdraws it on being assured unanimously that 'his services were of the utmost value'.

Basil was on the right side and it is to his credit that he understood and appreciated the new thinking, but he would never have been able, as his chairman was, to keep the support of his subscribers while leaving the changes to the inevitability of gradualness. He signed his last report as Chairman of the After-Care (Boys) Committee in 1961, a few months before he died.

The Jewish Board of Guardians

Basil had visited what is now the Jewish Welfare Board when first he was learning his work in Stepney; he soon joined them as a Visiting Guardian, working on the Industrial Committee at the apprenticing of boys, and being particularly concerned to find a method whereby a school-leaver of fourteen should have had enough time and opportunity to be sure that he really wanted to spend his life in the trade he was going to learn. He helped to create a Boys' Welfare Department. At one time he came near to resigning in a huff over the closing of a home for boys.

He comes out of the huff a little less than well. If he felt deeply about a matter he would sometimes take up a position not wholly within the bounds of what the facts would warrant, and when the facts were marshalled against him he would use a specious argument rather than retreat. This home had been founded by two dear friends, both killed in the First World War. In the Jewish Press he stated that the closing and the way it was carried out was a 'disgraceful episode'. His case was never very good on the merits; the better opinion seems to have been that the home had outlived its purpose. But the dispute, in public at least, turned on a paltry point of procedure which he could not successfully argue and should never have taken.

He did resign in 1958 after nearly forty years' work in one way or another for the welfare of the Board's youthful clients, and one may be sure it was done with enthusiasm backed by knowledge and understanding, even if he occasionally chose to bat on a bowler's wicket. When he died the Board gratefully acknowledged his services and their loss.

Other Causes or Matters

There were many other causes, less time-consuming, but all involving duties—more or less humble—which he laid upon himself.

Boots, for example. He was President of a school boot fund and wrote in 1936, 'I have been distributing boots for 21 years.' This was part of a long correspondence, extending over ten years, in which he was complaining in characteristic language, that the boots supplied 'are amazingly bad, lasting scarcely a month and the leather more like brown paper than leather'. The correspondence does not show that the accusation was conclusively proved.

Then there was the British Legion; he helped to re-found the St George's branch. He wrote, 'I was impressed by the fact that the renewal of a branch of the Legion containing men of all denominations would be all to the good in the present tense atmosphere of the district.' This was at the time when the British Union of Fascists were marching in the East End. The branch, when formed, wrote to thank him for his 'very great help in this matter'.

An extract from one of his letters to *The Times* shows an interest in young seafarers:

> In a large liner there are often as many as thirty lads between the ages of 14 and 19, fine adventurous boys, for whose moral, intellectual and physical welfare no one person is responsible . . . the NABC has been endeavouring to organise boys' clubs on these ships . . . In the very few cases in which it has succeeded the effect upon the characters of the boys has been amazing. They have been kept happy on board; they have been kept morally safe in foreign ports.

Delinquency could spring from unoccupied minds; his probationers must therefore have a nourishing mental diet. At once a scheme was devised to provide each of the probation officers with a collection of about fifty books, such as the age-groups eight to seventeen might enjoy, which could be lent to them without formality. The borough librarians co-operated nobly and made the scheme work. Within six months the Juvenile Courts Probation Officers, through their Society, told Basil that the scheme was successful and the probationers enthusiastic.

He was disturbed by the long hours which boys had to work, and an Act had been passed limiting their weekly hours. He wrote to the London Confederation of Boys' Clubs: 'I do feel that it is essential that clubs should see that none of their members are being made to work in places where the employer infringes the Act. I have just started a round-up in the club here and I am astonished at the number of boys who are made to work in shops for more than 52 hours a week.' There follows a scheme by which club managers are to ring up the Public Control Department of the LCC (number and extension given) whenever they find that a boy is working more than the prescribed hours.

He created and was chairman of a Group of the Hospital Saving Association, in his synagogue, and tried hard to rescue another which was in difficulties. The Association thanked him 'for the time you have devoted to these difficult conundrums and for your help and advice'. His own Group appears to have been successful because he wrote to the Association, 'Your Tuesday collection is creating a blockage of traffic in the corridors of the Settlement.'

He would never have claimed that he was doing anything more than his bare duty in reacting ferociously to anti-semitism, but with his immense work-load he deserves some credit for finding the time not merely for protesting but for probing into the causes and circumstances of each case and perhaps suggesting a remedy. He fought it without fear or favour, even when he thought he saw it in one whom he so much liked and respected as Sir W. Clarke Hall. That incident is a good example of his method. A Jewish employer in the East End had prosecuted his domestic servant, a young country girl, for stealing. In acquitting her the judge used strong language about 'aliens' who ill-treat their servants. Basil, after a fairly long and laborious probe, put his case and ended with the words: 'Although I know only too well that anti-semitism is the last thing that can be said of you the general public, who know you less well, may not have the same opinion', to which Clarke Hall answered, 'I am grateful for your kind suggestion and will bear it in mind.' The probe had revealed that for the last fifty years it had been the custom of Prison After-Care authorities throughout most of the United Kingdom to send young girls on discharge to certain parts of the country where 'rough work' was available and that a sort of traffic had grown up between those parts and London whereby these girls, or their descendants, would find their way back and obtain situations, sometimes in the East End, often resulting in friction or dismissal, a state of affairs to which both sides generally contributed. Practical suggestions followed, such as a conference of all concerned, church people from districts where the girls came from, small employers, including Jews from London, and social workers; after which an approach might be made to the relevant episcopal see.

That was good work and he did much of it. Sometimes he went off, as the saying is, at half-cock by impatiently misconstruing a phrase. But he was given to speaking intemperately.

To have the Care Committees at his elbow was very useful to Basil. There were fourteen schools in the district with nearly 9,000 pupils of whom some 5,400 were Jewish. He was a manager of some of them and was well aware how closely related they were to the welfare of his boys. He concerned himself more with morals and manners than with the curriculum. 'Sex matters should be cut out of it. They cause too much mischief; they are discussed so freely among teenagers that sex has gone to the heads of many of them.' The school leaving age was then fourteen and that would be the end of a boy's compulsory schooling unless he could qualify by examination for a free place in a fee-paying school.

In 1924 an Unemployment Insurance Bill was before Parliament and the leaving age, the age of insurability, maintenance grants and Day Continuation Schools were being debated. All these matters were of concern to Basil. He had seen the minds of his boys and girls applied to work and play in his club and knew what another year's teaching could do for them; he knew also what it meant to the parents to forgo the benefit of the boy's earning powers and therefore also the importance of unemployment insurance for school-leavers. A sub-committee of the Joint Council of London Juvenile Organisations Committees went to the House to put their suggestions to the Government. Basil writes in his diary:

Went with a deputation to H.A.L. Fisher[9] at the House of Commons re raising the school age to 15; Oyler, Eagar, Geoghan, Samuel and I. Masterman, Fisher and Lief Jones listened very patiently. Raising the school age would cost £7 million. Fisher was all for Day Continuation Schools[10] being revived. He thought work and school combined really excellent and was against boys kicking their heels at school until they got a job.

9

1939 to 1945.
The Settlement Carries On

When war was declared Basil applied to the War Office for registration in the Army Officers Emergency Reserve, but he was classed as unfit for active service because he had contracted diabetes. He enrolled in the Civil Defence Corps and together with Bunny set about adapting the Settlement to the conditions of total war.

There were many problems. The upper floors would be unsafe for Club use in case of air raids, the maintenance men would be called up, the Play Centre and older school children would be evacuated, and funds would drop because donations would be diverted to war charities. The Old Boys and Old Girls would be in the forces and only the younger working boys and girls would remain to use the safe parts of the building.

Fire-fighting apparatus was installed and its use practised, and gas-masks were distributed. Rooms in the basement were requisitioned by the Civil Defence Controller for the office of a District Warden and he and his company moved in at once. Club members of the Stepney No.1 Company Girls Training Corps acted as his messengers and as fire watchers throughout the night. Their tour of duty ended at 7a.m. after which most of them went to work. Basil, after training by the District Warden, undertook to be responsible for the air raid precautions. The basement could be used for shelter, and boys and girls were packed in tight to sleep on the floor of the synagogue head to tail so that they should not have to use the public shelters. Basil had to supervise the orderly occupation of this dormitory and then to take charge of the fire-fighting team on the roof. When more shelter space had been strengthened three more clubs (Brady Street, Stepney and Victoria) were invited to use it, and by a letter to *The Times* the secretary of the Association for Jewish Youth made it known that all clubs irrespective of creed would be welcomed at the Settlement.

As soon as the building had been put on a war footing Basil decided to resume Club activities for the remnant of the membership, using the large hall on the ground floor which was within easy reach of the shelters. There had been no more inflexible opponent of mixed clubs than Basil but it was not the time for bigotry and he had the courage to open an 'Oxford and St George's War Emergency Mixed Club'. His colleague on the NABC, W. McG. Eagar—not always uncritical of Basil—wrote to him, 'You are the youngest of us all, you are not too old to learn or to unlearn. Better heresies of doctrine than heresies of heart.' It began with 450 enrolments, the ages ranging from thirteen to forty. They were the London-based remnants of all the clubs and carried on as well as they could the peace-time routine. Six boys and six girls were elected 'House Captains'; on some nights boys and girls would be separated, on others they would spend the evening together. It worked well. Bunny could not give her whole time to this work. There was a call for women to volunteer to take charge of ambulance stations and since she could drive a car and was qualified to give first aid she thought she had a duty to the district to help it in its defence against enemy action. She was put in charge of the fire station at Cannon Street Road where she could do her duty by the station and yet give some time to the Settlement. Basil thought it was not enough and there was a furious row.

When members of the Club were called up they would come and say good-bye to Basil who would take each one, boy or girl, into the Synagogue and bless them. They would write to him as soon as they got to their unit and he would reply at once, but by October there were fifty serving members, and he and Sydney Franklin decided to revive the magazine *Fratres*[1] in which extracts from letters would be printed and a copy sent to every serving member. An Old Boy, a printer by trade, printed it at cost price, another designed the cover. Every issue contained an editorial homily, a list of serving members, home news and extracts from letters, and a prayer from Basil's *Prayers for Trench and Base*. Basil himself continued throughout the war to answer every letter which he received from Club members in the forces.

A war-time routine began to establish itself during which Basil supervised generally leaving the execution of the work in the charge of two trusted adjutants.[2] Rooms were used from which shelters could be easily reached when sirens sounded, and four Old Boys formed a panel of Air Raid Stewards. In an interview with a reporter from the *Star* Basil said: 'few people can realise the danger of the dark nights to boys and girls. It is essential to keep clubs open for their recreational facilities and for their work in moulding mind, body and character . . . Conditions are so bad that it is not safe for girls to go home alone. We have arranged for our girls to be accompanied.'

A new club was formed for boys between thirteen and fourteen who met every night except at weekends. A small voluntary school for twelve children was opened for an hour a day. They were not downhearted; a New Year dance was held and the Festival of Dedication[3] was appropriately celebrated by Old Boys and Old Girls in uniform. By April 1940 the Mixed Club had 900 members. They were kept in good heart by appreciative visitors. Twelve Protestant Canadian Chaplains who spent the night with them wrote, 'We all received much inspiration in witnessing the work you are doing and in sharing your worship'; the Bishop of Willesden spent an evening with them and gave them his blessing. The Civil Defence Artists' Exhibition of War Pictures, which was held monthly in a commercial gallery, was put on in the large hall of the Settlement where it was honoured by a visit from HM the Queen.

In October 1940, when the air raids had begun, an extract from *Fratres* under the caption 'Club News' gives a picture of life at the Settlement.

About 150 come to the Settlement every night. We have an ordinary Club evening of games until we descend to the shelters as the sirens go at dusk. On one night we have an impromptu concert, on another a debate . . . Around the building there are patrols throughout the night in two-hour watches with three fire-observers ready to give warning of incendiary bombs. We still keep the register but many go to the public shelters with their families . . . During the day the clothing depot which has been established here is used for those in need. A constant stream of people come for advice and help. Unemployed [sc. those who have time to spare] go to rest centres to offer any help they can. On weekends the club is open all day. The East End has had it badly and any number of members are unable to live in their homes, but not once has a wailing note been heard.

This account scarcely reveals the considerable scale on which clothing and food were distributed from the Settlement, clothing to the bombed-out and food to such shelters as had no canteens. It had begun as a voluntary unaided soup-round started by Bunny, typical of her improvisations. 'Hundreds of gallons of hot soup were carried round to the shelters each night . . . not only to the shelters but to firemen directing their hoses onto the blazing buildings. In addition chunks of sandwiches with hot fillings were popped into their mouths because they could not take their hands off the hoses.'[4]

At first the soup was brought in tea-urns slung between two people 'as at Camp'; after a time the urns and mugs and sandwiches were put in a box and tied to a delivery-boy's decrepit tricycle. In 1941 a permit to draw supplies for the making of the soup and sandwiches was granted by the Ministry of Food, who followed it in 1943 with the issue of a mobile canteen. What began as a modest 'soup-round' had proved its worth.

On behalf of the British Legion Major Sir J. Brunel Cohen[5] undertook to supply the Settlement with blankets for shelterers, clothing vouchers for the families of men and women in the services, travel vouchers for serving men and women to visit one another and a float of money to be applied at discretion. Gifts of blankets and much prized quilts of 'patch-work' came from Canada and 'Bundles for Britain' from America. Huge supplies of clothing were received for distribution to air raid victims. The whole of the Girls' Club floor was used . . . Many of the white blankets were made up into sleeping bags for the hundreds of babies who were brought into the shelters. Nearly all the work of storing and checking as well as of the actual distribution was done by Club and Settlement members. It was a tough piece of war-work which other clubs in Stepney did, perhaps on a smaller scale but with equal courage and perseverance. A Club school for unevacuated children was started at the Settlement; thirty-six boys aged from nine to thirteen attended regularly from 2 to 4; those from six to nine came in the morning and there was an evening school for boys between twelve and thirteen on weekdays.

Then there were the public shelters. 'Mr. Basil Henriques, Warden of the Jewish Settlement, had just been officiating at the wedding of one of the boys in his Club, now in the Army. Scarcely had the bridal couple driven off when he was off again in a white heat of energy and anger about the conditions in one of the big shelters.'[6] So wrote Mr (now Lord) Ritchie Calder in an article to the Press. The shelters were grossly overcrowded and the latrines were too near the canteens, which were little more than a ring-burner and a tap. The arches of the viaduct that carries the railway eastward over Mark Lane, known as the 'Tilbury' (it used to be the London, Tilbury and Southend Railway) were scheduled as a public shelter. He took Kingsley Martin, of the *New Statesman*, and Lady Limerick, head of the London Branch of the Red Cross, to see the overcrowding and the need for a first-aid post and medical supervision. It was a useful visit because in due course an aid post was installed where Basil's niece, Esmé Henriques, was on duty. Martin wrote an article about it in the *New Statesman* which some considered actionable by Stepney Borough Council. When it was rumoured that the unscheduled arches of the 'Tilbury' were to be closed Basil went to the Home Office and warned Miss Ellen Wilkinson[7] that there would be a riot if the people were turned out. Eventually it had to be closed because an unexploded bomb had lodged in the roof.

His next concern was for the effect on youth of the use of public shelters, where theft, looting and promiscuity were difficult to prevent. He wrote to the Department of Home Security pointing out that his Settlement had spent £320 on strengthening the part used by the Clubs and that if more rooms were strengthened by the local authority there would be no need to limit accommodation to their own club members, of whom some 150 to 200 spent every evening there, slept and had supper and breakfast. The matter went on to Sir Henry Willink, the Special Commissioner for Re-Housing, and eventually the Borough Council did the necessary strengthening. The Settlement was classified as a public shelter, but was reserved by ticket for members of boys' and girls' clubs, and comparable organisations. A committee set up by the Church of England Temperance Society, consisting of clergymen, doctors and social workers, under the chairmanship of Basil, made a survey of 150 London shelters and found that only a few of them were fit for young people; their suggestions were passed on to Whitehall. The provision of Youth Recreation Centres was due to the combined efforts of the National Associations of Boys' Clubs and Girls' Clubs respectively as well as the free-lance work of Basil, who had been pleading for such measures since the outbreak of war; the Centres were for young people awaiting call-up who did not belong to any youth-group and their purpose was to keep them happily occupied and out of mischief. Basil declared that if boys and girls of the sixteen to eighteen age group were compelled to join a youth-group it would stem the flow of delinquents.

Although his work as Warden was physically more tiring and his hours on the Bench longer he never gave up his prison visiting or his work for the Norwood Home and the London Hospital. He gave his nightly religious talk at 'Time' and took a good share of the preaching in the Synagogue. And, of course, there was always *Fratres*. Lest any possible Settlement war-potential should go unexploited he formed a company of Army Cadets, enrolled as E Coy., 1st Bn The Royal Fusiliers Cadets; they drilled in the roof gymnasium and the Old Boys were officers with Basil in command.

But it was getting too much for him. Bunny writes, 'Complete exhaustion overwhelmed him in the latter part of 1942 which necessitated a few days' complete rest under doctor's orders.' The tonic that set him up again was a call to lecture in America on behalf of the Ministry of Information.[8]

He flew over in April 1943 and returned at the end of June well and in good spirits. Bunny writes:

He arrived safely and immediately produced a magnificent petticoat for me which he said cost 25 dollars at the smartest ladies' outfitting shop. After touring the building from roof garden to basement workshop he tried to write letters of thanks to America and to compile his reports for the M. o I . . . The evenings belonged to the clubs and cadets.

By way of getting into his stride he took the cadet company to camp at Southcourt,[9] where they slept in empty horse boxes and were given field training by regular N.C.O's. According to their officer's report 'their appearance was smart, their arms drill steady and good and their lay-out of kits excellent'.

He soon found that life on the Home Front gave him a great deal to say, and he somehow made the time to say it.

He went about the country telling people how the younger generation were behaving in war time, and what should be done for those of them who were still left in the big cities.

He was one of five speakers all in close touch with juveniles, who were asked to give their views on the state of juvenile delinquency. He said that in spite of an increase in delinquency (less among boys than girls) the youth of today were showing 'an unprecedented altruism and heroism'. At a meeting at the Croydon Town Hall, where he was guest-speaker, he said 'this country had been disgracefully behind others in Europe in recognising that our strength lies in youth. I remember how we talked of making England a land fit for heroes to live in after the last war. We are saying the same today. But what happened between the two wars? Is it a proud record? The school leaving age is the same. [It was 14] For twenty-five years we have let boys and girls go out into the world physically unfit for facing the hardships of factory life . . . Youth has never been grander in their attitude to war and to each other and in their desire to serve.'

In youth work he said educational authorities should co-operate with voluntary workers who could provide cultural and spiritual education. At Barrow he took part in the opening of the first camp for young people who were unattached to any group until called up; he had long been urging local authorities to provide such camps. At Cleckheaton he spoke on the breakdown of religion as the cause of crime among the young, and at the Greenwich Youth Committee on the 're-building job, or re-shaping the future of youth'. At Sheffield his subject was the danger of high wages for boys. 'Owing to the shortage of labour boys were earning men's wages, often for unskilled work in blind alley jobs. The boy becomes unstable; he goes from one job to another leaving one situation with the certainty of finding another.' He told the Rotarians at Cardiff that children should be treated as one treats hospital patients 'with the best equipment and staff available'.

That is how Basil and Bunny spent the war years and at the end they could look back with satisfaction at the part their Settlement had played. 665 Old Boys and Girls had served in the forces; 61 were commissioned, 171 became NCOs, 27 were killed. Of the commissioned officers 35 had been Club members as boys. Of 24 who were commissioned in the army 3 had had elementary education, 4 left a central school[10] at 15, 14 went to secondary school, and 3 got university degrees. All came from working class homes, all but one were Jews, all but one were children of foreign immigrant parents. The bulk of the army commissions were in the infantry and the artillery.[11] His mother's advice given some thirty years since that he would be able to 'anglicise' the children of immigrant Jewish parents, had proved to be right.

10

On the Warpath, or
the Technique of Making a Fuss

'I will drive my tank against evil wherever I find it.' So said Basil at a dinner given him by the Old Boys on an anniversary or some such occasion. The metaphor was apter than he thought. A tank on the attack is no respecter of persons, and may leave a trail of damage to the just as well as the unjust, to friends, to enemies or to mere strangers. So it was with Basil. Sometimes he did not seem to mind who got hurt on the way as long as he reached his objective.

He kept up a running battle with the Home Office over the disposal of the delinquent after committal, which involved remand homes, approved schools, classifying centres and 'closed houses' for persistent absconders. He disapproved, in dogmatic terms, of the centres; classifying, he thought, should be done in adequately manned and equipped remand homes, though weighty opinion among the magistrates disagreed with him. He wrote to a friend: 'My latest stunt is to show up the scandal of the delay at the Home Office' in designating the appropriate school after committal, although he was given what seem to be good and sufficient reasons for delay in each case. Of a project for 'closed annexes' in open schools he said, 'The Home Office have so far turned it down' when in fact they said they were considering it and experimenting with similar schemes.

Temperament and habit had made him that kind of a man. He was above all things ardent, and with his ardour went great moral courage. He had been ardent as a child, ardent enough to preach at the age of eight, then, as a schoolboy, to try himself out at lessons, games, music and literature, and when he had found his true bent he was ardent to put wrong right. Though astute and a good tactician he often seemed to have neither the wish nor the patience to analyse his opponent's case to any great depth, and if, as occasionally happened, the 'evil' which he set out to fight was merely something with which for the time being he happened to disagree, he was capable of using arguments which, as an old and irritated friend told him, were felt to be 'not cricket and unfair'.

Added to this was his habit of speaking in superlatives. As far back as his first address to the sponsoring synagogues C.G.M. had warned him about his prodigal use of 'awfully'. The habit grew on him and it seemed as if he sometimes let his words take charge of his thinking. People were 'indescribably saint-like' or 'abominable' or 'outstandingly brilliant' or 'incredibly stupid'; occasions were 'the finest hour in my life' or 'the most appalling evening I have ever spent'. The bodies corporate with whom he might find himself in controversy had no feelings to hurt, but friends would write to him sadly that the words he had used could only have been meant to break the friendship. Yet he was the kindest and most compassionate of men. The fact is that he liked to have his own way. One of the original members of the Club, than whom no other knew Basil better nor loved him more, said, 'everybody could work under him, nobody could work with him'. He could be a difficult team-mate, but a very benevolent despot.

It is doubtful whether he initiated any measures; he would find some fault or inadequacy in law or administrative procedure which was known to be in need of amendment, but where the movement for reform had lost its impetus and nothing much was being done. It needed somebody to make a fuss and Basil was their man. He would constitute himself the spearhead of the movement and attack on a wide front with incomparable élan.

That was the way he played his part in the amending of the procedure for taking the evidence of child witnesses.

Child Witnesses

Writing to Lord Longford in June 1961, Basil spoke of his 'new campaign'. A man who had been committed for trial some three months previously on a charge of sexually assaulting a little girl was acquitted because the girl, on being asked, said that she was not sure about the meaning of an oath. Basil wrote: 'I am so boiling with fury that I hardly know what to do.'

Ever since the report of the Departmental Committee on Sexual Offences against Young Persons in 1925[1] those actively interested in the moral and social welfare of children[2] and in the law relating thereto had been working to remedy the defects in procedure revealed in that report.

At the time of Basil's 'campaign' the problem, briefly put, fell under two main heads, viz. (i) the acquittal of guilty defendants because their victims were too young to give sworn evidence; (ii) the traumatic effect on the child of having to repeat the details of the event so that the case could be put before the court, coupled with the long delay if the accused should elect to be tried by jury, and the ordeal of the child in the witness box.

That is how it appeared to the 1925 Committee, and the Ingleby Committee on Children and Young Persons[3] which presented its report in October 1960 made recommendations with regard to the procedure with child witnesses calculated to avoid the harmful effects of which the earlier Committee had given clear warning. Five of Basil's colleagues in the Magistrates' Association had given evidence to the Ingleby Committee, and the Association, largely at Basil's instigation, had embodied their recommendations in a long and detailed report which was sent to the Home Office.[4]

The case at Quarter Sessions[5] referred to above which had made Basil 'boil with fury' occurred in 1961 and on 31 May he opened his 'new campaign' with a letter to *The Times* in which he described the 'fearful ordeal' of the sexually assaulted child who may have to describe the assault in detail five times in the course of three or four weeks, which made some parents so reluctant to prosecute that dangerous perverts might go unpunished. Instead of having to give evidence again at Quarter Sessions the child could be cross-examined on an affidavit made in the magistrate's court and for the avoidance of delay such cases should be treated as 'hospital emergency cases' and dealt with almost immediately so that 'what might have been a slight wound does not become a permanent scar'. He followed this up by writing to the Lord Chancellor[6] enclosing a copy of his letter to *The Times* and describing in detail the case at Sessions which had moved him so powerfully. He ended his letter with an appeal:

> If only these cases could be heard before a jury in a Juvenile
> Court room, with the Press present but with the Court
> having power to suppress the names of the child witnesses,[7]
> and if only the Chairman and Counsel did not wear wigs, and
> if only the Chairman were assisted by a member of a Juvenile
> Court panel, justice would be manifestly done!
> Furthermore it is of the utmost importance that the trial
> should take place as soon as possible after the alleged event.
> It seems incredible that in London there would be a delay of
> more than three months.[8]

A reply from the Lord Chancellor's office said that the letter raised important issues in the sphere of criminal procedure in cases where the strain on child witnesses would clearly be great, and that Basil's observations would be passed to the Children's Department of the Home Office who for their part assured him that his suggestions would be considered along with the Ingleby recommendations.

The next step was to enlist the support of the public by letters to the Press and to write personally to such individuals as had the power and influence to help in the cause.[9] He wrote describing the position with regard to child witnesses to eighteen newspapers including the national dailies and weeklies, the *Spectator,* the *New Statesman,* the *Tablet,* the *Church Times,* and the *Christian Scientist,* and from all of them he got sympathetic replies. In answer to a personal letter Lord Cohen of Walmer[10] said that it was 'an excellent presentation of the case'; Lord Denning[11] said: 'You always raise such good points. I feel that we ought to do something about these child witnesses'; Lord Birkett[12] wrote: 'I like to think you are in the world doing the kind of work that you are doing and keeping a vigilant eye on these matters.' Lady Adrian[13] agreed with the need for reform but thought that the Ingleby recommendations might solve the problem if only they were accepted by the lawyers[14] which she doubted. Mr Grimond[15] raised the matter in the House of Commons, Mr Chuter Ede,[16] Mr Jeremy Thorpe[17] and Mr Christopher Chataway expressed their warm support, and Lady Elliot of Harwood[18] said, 'You certainly are a most indefatigable person . . . I am entirely with you in what you write.'

And indeed he was indefatigable. There was scarcely a group of any standing in England interested even peripherally in the moral welfare of children to whom he did not write, and he received support from all of them.[19]

Some of the reforms were carried out but Basil did not live to see them. The form of oath for children has been altered to: 'I promise before Almighty God to tell the truth', though the other form may be administered;[20] a child may not be called before examining justices as a witness for the prosecution, but a written statement is admissible unless the accused objects or the child is needed to identify,[21] and the prohibition against publication of the child's identity is no longer confined to sexual cases but is of general application to child witnesses.[22]

The Boston Experiment

The campaign for the Attendance Centres, or the Boston experiment, followed the same pattern. In 1956 he had gone on a lecture tour to America at the instance of the British Council and had come back full of enthusiasm for the sort of quasi-penal establishment for young offenders which he had found working very successfully in Boston, Massachusetts.

He began with an article in the *Magistrate*, the journal of the Magistrates' Association, but although he succeeded in convincing both that body and the Probation Officers' Association of the virtues of the Boston model and of the need to introduce it or something like it in this country, no movement seems to have been started or much progress made. However, early in the year 1961 the Criminal Justice Bill (which was to become the Criminal Justice Act, 1961) was being introduced into Parliament; it dealt with custodial establishments for young offenders before and after committal. That was the time to act, and by way of a fanfare he opened his campaign with an article in *The Times* signed by himself and two fellow magistrates (Mr J. P. Marindin and Mrs Ursula Thorpe) which, here summarised, explains his purpose:

There are insufficient Detention Centres and the Borstals and Senior Approved Schools and Remand Centres are overfull. Something must be done to prevent this dangerous state of affairs. A form of treatment on the lines of the Boston Training Centre in America offers a solution. There are many under the age of 21 who require something more than straightforward probation but who do not need a long and expensive residential training away from home. Young offenders would be sent voluntarily as a condition of their probation (just as they are now sent to an Approved School or Home) to the proposed Centre, where they would have to spend two hours of their leisure on every weekday for three months, at the end of which time they would report back to the Court either to continue their probation in the ordinary way, or be ordered some form of residential training if they have done badly at the Centre or to be discharged if they have done exceptionally well.

The advantages are
a It is much cheaper than residential training.
b The offenders remain at home and the parents are encouraged to co-operate with the staff in training their sons.
c The Probation Officer can study the probationer with other boys.
d Psychological treatment is available.
e In 130 hours some constructive reformative treatment has a chance of being achieved.

He then wrote to the Home Secretary (Mr R. A. Butler as he then was) asking him to incorporate the scheme into the Bill, and was told that the Minister intended to reserve judgment on the proposal pending a full examination into the questions of principle and the practical problems to which it gave rise. In the meanwhile the Minister offered to discuss it with the Magistrates' Association.

Thereupon Basil tried to outflank the Home Office by an attack through the House of Commons in the course of which he captured no less a person than Mr Chuter Ede, who agreed to move an amendment introducing a clause under which the scheme could be tried out. This was followed by letters to MPs asking them to be present in the House to support the amendment and at the same time, by way of getting support in the constituencies for members who might vote for the amendment, he wrote again to the Press, this time to the *Daily Telegraph*, in which he neatly used the current alarm about vandalism in railway carriages to point out that there would be no vandalism if there were adequate training centres for the reformation of juvenile offenders, and that the amendment standing in Mr Chuter Ede's name would provide the very remedy in the form of training centres of the Boston pattern where 'social group loyalty could be instilled to take the place of their anti-social behaviour'.

Alas, the amendment was 'not called' in the Commons and Basil's only chance was to have a similar one moved when the Bill reached the House of Lords. Having persuaded Lord Longford to move it he called up his reserves whom he rallied by a letter to the *Manchester Guardian*, although he said he was 'depressed' and 'infuriated' by the attitude of the Press and complained that in reporting the Bill they had given nearly all the space to corporal punishment and little or none to his training centres. In fact the *Manchester Guardian* gave him a short leader pressing for the inclusion of enabling powers in the Bill. He then wrote to both Archbishops, the Bishops of London, Norwich and Sheffield, the Lord Chief Justice, Lords Goddard and Denning, Lord Justice Devlin, as he then was, ten peers, including Lord James of Rusholme, High Master of Manchester Grammar School, and two peeresses. Lady Elliot of Harwood and Lady Wootton of Abinger. They all promised support if they could manage to be present. He made a bid for academic approval by writing to Professor Radzinowicz, of the Cambridge Institute of Criminology, who, however, warily replied that he was a member of the Home Office Advisory Council where he would have an opportunity of making himself more familiar with the scheme which he was being asked to support.

Lord Longford moved his amendment with a powerful and persuasive presentation of the case, and was supported by the Bishop of Exeter, Lords Meston, Ailwyn, Stonham, and James of Rusholme, and Lady Wootton of Abinger. However, the Lord Chancellor, Lord Kilmuir, speaking without hostility to the scheme, built up a well-founded case that more 'legislative background' was required before enabling powers could be introduced. Perhaps he was merely saying that the Home Office was not going to be bounced, Archbishops or no, but in the face of his very reasonable arguments the amendment was withdrawn. The upshot was that the scheme was referred by the Home Secretary to his Advisory Council on Juvenile Offenders, who appointed a special sub-committee to consider Basil's proposals and other schemes for non-residential training. Lady Elliot of Harwood was appointed chairman.

In his speech Lord Longford had said, 'No name commands more widespread admiration in his field than that of Sir Basil Henriques, although he would be the first to disclaim the personal credit which he deserves for bringing this plan so forcibly before the minds of the public.' He was right. Basil had a genius for bringing things forcibly before people's minds, and admiration was there in plenty. Besides the Bishops, there were judges, recorders, and magistrates, people whose profession it was to understand such matters, who praised him warmly for his 'excellent' scheme and wished it well. What perhaps may have pleased him most was the last sentence of a letter from Lady Elliot of Harwood after she had been appointed chairman in which she outlined her plans for the working of her sub-committee: 'I thought you would like to know that your efforts started the ball rolling.'

The Jewish Fellowship

The ideas for which the Fellowship was to stand did not originate with Basil. There was a minority which mistrusted as profoundly as he did—and for the same reasons—the course on which in 1942 the Jewish community was being set, but they had neither formed a party nor started any movement. Basil determined to give them a collective voice and to make it heard.

At the heart of the matter was a politico-religious problem which had its roots so far back in antiquity that the general reader requires the help of a few flashbacks by which to see the picture albeit in the barest outline and with many gaps.

About the end of the second century the struggle to regain national independence in Palestine seemed to be lost and thereafter Judaism connoted a religion and not a political entity. Prayers for the promised coming of the Kingdom of God on earth had indeed always had a place in the liturgy. 'Gather our exiles from the four corners of the earth and lead us exulting to Zion thy city' were sentiments uttered by traditional Jews with the utmost sincerity but believed with no less sincerity to relate to a Messianic era when, and only when, the worship of God should be universal. Until then—so it was taught—it was wrong to try to put last things first. Yet wherever there was persecution the hope persisted.

At the close of the nineteenth century Theodor Herzl founded the Zionist movement. It was born of anti-semitism ranging from the brutal to the barely perceptible but nowhere wholly stamped out, and it proclaimed that to anticipate the Messianic dispensation with a 'legally assured home in Palestine' was not only pardonable but praiseworthy. Its numbers increased after the Balfour Declaration and, later, with the achievements of the settlers under the Mandate. Its song was called 'The Hope'.

Finally, during the Nazi persecutions, even before the gas chambers had been publicised, many, perhaps most, Jews were disposed to be receptive to a call, if it should come, for nationalism in their time. It came in 1941 from Dr Weizmann, the Zionist leader, and was for 'the setting up of a Jewish state in Palestine as part of a general peace settlement'.

That minority, however, of which Basil was one was not so receptive. Ideologically it comprised two main groups: there were the Progressives (i.e. the Reform and Liberal congregations) whose Judaism had always been universalist, and there were traditional Jews (some of them very strict in their religious practices) who held fast to the old doctrine of Messianism. It was a fair cross-section of the community, ordinary folk with a sprinkling of the eminent: rabbis, judges, bankers, scholars, scientists, and industrialists.[23] The common bond was the fear that nationality would supplant religion as the criterion of what was Jewish.

So in 1942 he founded his Fellowship 'because', he says, 'there was no other organisation in Anglo-Jewry which stood for the same things as the Fellowship wanted to promote'. He was at first trying not to start a new movement but merely to build up a non-Zionist fellowship of Jews who justified their Judaism by their religion. He was keeping his movement on the stocks, as he said, until the time was ready to launch it. On his American tour in 1943 he did his best to spread the Fellowship doctrine. 'At a party at Rabbi X's I addressed them on the Fellowship . . . I had some opposition from those of extreme Zionist views.' There was a parallel movement, the American Council for Judaism. Basil says, 'Their enthusiasm was tremendous. They were fearless and there was no sitting on the fence . . . They tried to exclude proposals to deal with Central European Jews, but they produced a bold fine document on the Jews as a religious community.'

He had lunch with Arthur Sultzberger of the *New York Times*. 'The difference between the N.Y.T. lunch and New Court[24] was that there was no side-talking, the speaker for the time being monopolising the whole conversation; but the food was as good as New Court at its best except that there was milk instead of wine . . . He impressed me by his sincerity and integrity . . . we discussed the Fellowship and the American movement of which I hope he will be Vice-President.'

He launched his movement in November 1944; its president was Sir J. Brunel Cohen.

Basil was astute enough to see that his movement would not thrive on mere negation. Its first purpose, he said, was to strengthen the religious life of Anglo-Jewry; its basic principles were that the Jews were a people bound together by their religion, history and tradition, that it rejected the idea of a separate political Jewish nationality and that there could be no substitute for Judaism in the life of the Jewish people. Its method was to be 'by means of meetings, conferences, publications and local organisations. Above all it will mobilise the Jewish youth for service to Anglo-Jewry in its religious life'.

It went seriously to work. It published three pamphlets setting out its principles and its aims, and the 'challenge' to every Jew to decide whether he was a Jew by religion or nationality.

With a following so various in its religious attitudes he had to be latitudinarian. There was a tract on Judaism and another on the Sabbath, each giving two views: the one Progressive by Basil, the other, traditional by an orthodox scholar. In consultation with scholars on both sides he wrote a tract on the dietary laws which was, for him, temperate and fair.[25] Meetings were held in London, Manchester and Birmingham. A very competent journalist was employed and publicity was ensured by 'Information Bulletins' and by a monthly publication called the *Outlook*. By sponsoring the publication of the *Journal of Jewish Studies* the Fellowship helped to revive the Biblical and religious scholarship which had formerly been the content of the *Jewish Quarterly Review*.

In January 1946, an Anglo-American Commission of Enquiry on European Jewry and Palestine presided over by Mr Justice Singleton, as he then was, was holding its sittings in London and among those who gave evidence were the Board of Deputies and the Anglo-Jewish Association.[26] The latter, however, declined to put forward the views of the Fellowship, which was therefore allowed to give its own evidence. It was pleaded by the Fellowship's representative[27] that the Board had been captured by a Zionist caucus so that it no longer represented Anglo-Jewry and that the extent to which the Fellowship had been misrepresented in the Jewish Press made it necessary to give evidence to the Commission. And indeed they were misrepresented both in and out of the Press. Basil was 'the Jewish anti-semite', 'the man who stabbed Zionism in the back', 'the traitor', 'the cold-hearted snob indifferent to the sufferings of foreign Jews'.

118

By this time they were about 1,500 strong, and were increasing but very slowly; 'a small figure, yet considering the handicaps we have faced and the shortness of time not entirely unsatisfactory'. Reporting on the work of the deputation Basil said, 'we can now hope that we may be able to drop our public work and get down in all seriousness to our real purpose, which is to strengthen the religious life of all sections of Jewry in this country.'

But events overtook them. In 1948 the State of Israel was proclaimed, and after a short period of indecision the prevailing Jewish mood was 'the state must not fail'. There could no longer be any opposition to it, and, what was a determining factor, the funds, energy and enthusiasm which might have helped the Fellowship were devoted to the new State of Israel. In November 1948 the Fellowship was wound up.

Writing about their appearance before the Anglo-American Commission Basil had said, 'No one else stood up and said that our nationality is British, that there is no such thing as a Jewish nation, that we are Jews by the faith which we possess and that we are not political exiles awaiting repatriation to a Jewish state.' It was he who stood up and said it and got the brickbats. Yet he had caused the conscientious objections to Jewish nationalism to be forcefully and reasonably publicised, and without him a group of British Jews who by virtue of their religious convictions, their character, attainments and public service had a right to be heard would have had no collective voice.

11

Leisure, Holidays and Busmen's Holidays

Leisure

Throughout their working life Basil and Bunny enjoyed the modest pleasures proper to what their parents would have called polite society; the rule under which they lived imposed no asceticism except hard work and long hours.

At first Basil used to play squash in the Settlement court and tennis at Southcourt where they would go most weekends, often with one or two boys or girls from the Club, for recreation or the preparing of sermons or just to sleep.

> Gardened all day.
> Played tennis hard all day.
> Dug and mowed all day, very delightful.
> Sermon, potatoes, patience.

Patience was used as a sedative to which he had become an addict; he played it whenever he was too tired to think.

They had their 'evenings out'.

> Went with B to movies.
> Went with B to see the *Eternal Flame* at the Empire.
> Went to *Hänsel and Gretel;* delightful, I thoroughly enjoyed it.
> Went to Syb's dance.
> Dinner at the Grocers' Company in their Hall; ate every course and thoroughly enjoyed it.

And by day

> Went to Lords to see England v. Australia; very restful and enjoyable.

Went with B to see Italian pictures at Burlington House;
somehow it was all too rich. Besides, the London
atmosphere compared to the Florentine does not help me to
appreciate pictures.
Lunched at the Troc with B; bought a new hat, went to the
movies in Coventry Street, tea at the Corner House.

Then there was the Reform Club. He used it mostly for
lunchtime discussions of his own subjects—youth service,
delinquency, religion—with knowledgeable people for whom it
would be a more convenient meeting place than St
George's-in-the-East. He rarely went there alone, but there is an
entry in 1923:

Went down to Dover to see Brodie [a Chaplain to the Forces
and later Chief Rabbi] off. Felt very sad at losing one of the
dearest friends I have made. Came back immediately and
dined at the Reform alone.

Holidays

They had a few holidays abroad, to Italy, Egypt, Ceylon, the
Mediterranean, South Africa, and the West Indies, and Basil
went on a trip to Norway as C. G. M.'s guest. They conform,
more or less, to a general pattern. The holiday is taken because
both of them are tired out and cannot go on any longer, so that
they have to forgo the anticipatory pleasure of planning their
tour and, instead, have it done for them by a travel agent. When
they arrived, however, they would find that others had done
some planning; somebody had written about them to a
governor or a consul or a chief magistrate or the association of
club leaders or a probation officer or a business nabob and, of
course, to any Old Boy or Old Girl of O.St.G. who had settled
there. Thus at Colombo (1936): 'Arrived at 6 a.m. and was told
that four people were waiting to receive us, in the saloon. They
were C -, G - and R - of Toc H and X - of the Ceylon Police Force
who had been to the Settlement.' X's chief, the Inspector
General, sent his launch for them: 'he had gone to great lengths
to plan our tour for us'. So of course they went to a Police Club

'run exactly on N.A.B.C. lines'. The Governor asked them to lunch, 'very formal but very jolly'. The social conscience moved him occasionally to comment disapprovingly on what they see, perhaps with something of the easy self-assurance of the outsider. 'Went to a tea-factory; very upset at the slavery of the women sorting the tea'; Bunny said they were singing. Facts about the industry now widely known suggest that he may have felt that things were different below the surface.

On their way back through Bombay they were met by an Indian doctor (it was part of the planning) who had met them in London at a Liberal Jewish conference, so Basil had to preach in the Liberal Jewish Synagogue.

The South African tour (1938-9) was described by Bunny as a 'deliberately planned busman's holiday', but it was a holiday as well. They were met at Cape Town by an Old Boy (he had played Hans Sachs in Bunny's production of *Meistersinger* at the Settlement), and in due course went visiting boys' clubs, industrial schools, hostels and housing estates, and he addressed native leaders. They were given a civic lunch by the Mayor of Johannesburg, and invited to lunch with the Governor and his wife (Sir Patrick and Lady Duncan). Bunny met some cousins and Basil his nephew Lionel. They were lucky to have Sir George Albu, President of the South African Association of Boys' Clubs, generously overseeing their comforts throughout the tour. Old Boys and Girls gave them a send-off at Cape Town.

In September 1927 Basil had come back from camp 'exhausted' and next day said to Bunny at breakfast 'let's go on a short holiday'. Cooks arranged it and they were on board next day bound for Naples so that there was no time for anybody to write to anybody. They climbed up Vesuvius and down into the crater, explored Pompeii—'wonderful beyond words'—and then on to Rome, Florence, Siena, San Gimignano, Venice and then home. He expressed himself about the artifacts. At Florence, 'Uffizi all the morning until nearly sick with wonder'; 'St. Marco monastery, full of Fra Angelico and Savonarola, the best thing in Florence'. At Venice, 'Not thrilled by Venetian school, even the Bellini and Tintoretto, but enchanted by the Church of the Frari, with Titian's Assumption as altar piece, a perfect Bellini Madonna in sacristy, Titian's mausoleum and

Canova's tomb.' The Lido, however, aroused the social conscience: 'revolted beyond all words by depravity of society in silk pyjamas and perverted style of amusements.'

On all his journeys since boyhood he had taken a delight in landscape. 'Glorious natural harbour' at Toulon; 'Indescribably beautiful drive to Amalfi.' On the trip to Norway he wrote, 'I was struck by the exceptional brilliance of the green grass and the masses of kingcups' and, as they waited up to see the midnight sun, 'The next twenty minutes were some of the most glorious I have ever experienced. The mountains became a deep red from the rays of the sun which was about 2 diameters above the horizon and then gradually after midnight they assumed a cold grey until they became red again from the dawn. It was a breathless experience and quite indescribable. Went to bed feeling drunk with wonder.'

Busmen's Holidays

At the instance of the British Council Basil went on lecture tours in America, Australia, the West Indies and Sweden. Of the long and detailed diaries which he kept only such excerpts have been included here as illustrate his character and point of view. Much of the contents might in fact be useful for research into the social services of those countries at that time. Whether or to what extent he had any influence on the course taken by youth movements of the countries he visited it is impossible to assess. The service of youth was everywhere experimental and transitional, so that changes which may have taken place after his visits are not necessarily to be ascribed to them. What does emerge with certainty is that on the subjects of boys' clubs and juvenile delinquency he was heard with respect in three continents.

America 1943

Early in 1943 Basil was asked to go on a lecture tour in the United States on behalf of the Ministry of Information acting with the Home Office and the American Embassy. Leaving

123

Bernard Prins and Sydney Franklin to edit *Fratres* he flew out in a bomber on 1 April. By the time he returned nearly twelve weeks later he had travelled from New York to Washington, then south to Los Angeles and so back to Baltimore and Boston, visiting seventeen cities and making forty speeches, mostly on problems of childhood and adolescence, occasionally on Britain in wartime or on Progressive Judaism. He kept a diary from which some extracts are chosen to show his energy and his moods. Thus, at Seattle: 'Gave several interviews. Attended Washington State Conference on Social Work—first session "the child in wartime" . . . Lunched with the President of the Conference and others. Had to give a short address followed by questions. The Sheriff was greatly disturbed by the moral degeneration of the young . . . Gave a public address to the State Conference at which the Mayor was present. The Hall was packed—about 700 present. Spoke for an hour and got a tremendous reception . . . Had to go on to a private house but I was so exhausted I could have shrieked, but I revived after some milk and bread' or 'I addressed the State Conference of Probation Officers for 70 minutes, and had a terrific reception; I let myself go.' Of his visit to the Judge Baker Guidance Centre he says: 'It was the most important address of my tour, for there is no greater authority in the world on juvenile delinquency than the staff of the clinic, headed by Dr Healey and his wife . . . fortunately I was in good form . . . the applause was embarrassingly long and so was my speech.' He preached, he gave Press conferences and he broadcast; on hearing a record of one of his broadcasts he wrote, 'I sound like a very old, pompous and sanctimonious man.'

He gives us a bird's-eye view of the American system of dealing with juvenile offenders as it was some thirty years ago, with some characteristic comments. Of the City Prison, Seattle: 'The lack of privacy seems awful; nowhere to cry, nowhere to pray alone, nowhere to repent, nowhere to make amends . . . all ages are there from 16 upwards . . . nothing to do except infect each other's morals; no outdoor exercise, no reformative or constructive work; no Discharged Prisoners Aid . . . Kitchens magnificent and food excellent.'

Of the Federal Prison on McNiel Island: 'A model prison . . .

The Governor has great human understanding . . . A prisoner remains quarantined for thirty days during which he is observed, tested and examined, so that the Governor can decide what work to put him to.'

Of the Portland (Oregon) juvenile court: 'The judge has a genius for his work . . . it is a privilege to see how he conducts his cases . . . The Probation officer discusses the child in his presence.'

Of the San Francisco juvenile court: 'Probation Officers visit the boys not vice versa, so that the probationers do not congregate and become known to each other . . . There is an excellent practice of trying an adult charged with an offence against a child in a juvenile court, so that the child does not have to give evidence in an adult court. This is better than in England.'

Of the Framington juvenile court: 'Atmosphere as in Toynbee Hall, combining informality and respect . . . Boys on probation attend two hours every week day to prove that they can be industrious, obedient and disciplined.'

Of the Framington Women's Reformation: 'The Governor is a lady of exceptional culture and charm . . . Her aim is to teach a love of beauty and that life can be beautiful. But there is little beauty about the place . . . The women seem fairly happy and respectful.'

In an extempore address at the Ministry of Justice in Washington he summarised his impression of the American system. 'The emphasis is on correction rather than prevention.'

But he always remained the leader of his Club. Old Boys of O.St.G. who were staying in America or had settled there travelled miles to see him. Of one such encounter he wrote:

> J.F. (O.St.G.) met me at the station . . . spent the evening reminiscing in his home, making all the family members as if it were an officers meeting . . . I felt I had spent a real club evening . . . He remembers the tiniest detail of his club life and has re-lived his youth with me. There must be few people who get so rewarded without merit as we are in the real love of the children, or who have the satisfaction of knowing that one's life has not been altogether spent in vain. It all makes me want to cry, in thankfulness and humility.

The danger of excessive humility was averted by a letter from the British Consul in Seattle: 'Yours has been an outstanding visit of which nothing but good has been heard.'

Australia

The Australian tour was in 1948 and this time Bunny went with him. They arrived in January and returned in June, having travelled over the whole country, and spent four weeks in New Zealand lecturing and broadcasting each on their own subjects, Bunny's being girls' clubs and all related problems, and her experiences in Germany after the war. As in America they visited most of the institutions to which young offenders are brought and learnt something about the system of dealing with them.

In Sydney he encountered the Child Welfare Department and its Director and wrote:

> This is one of the most remarkable men I have ever met . . .
> He has conceived and put into practice the *ideal* system for
> child welfare well ahead even of the recommendations of the
> Curtis Report . . . It does all the preventative work as well as
> the reformative . . . All errants are dealt with by him . . . If
> poverty is the cause he is able to arrange relief, and his
> department deals with all matrimonial and affiliation cases,
> as well as adoption . . . A man of vision, initiative, wisdom,
> understanding of human nature (and especially of children)
> and administrative ability . . . It is essential that Britain
> catches up with this most brilliant scheme. Either we should
> get Hicks over to us or R (of the Home Office) should come
> over here.

This was in 1948 and he developed it in *The Home-Menders* in 1955. There are to be offices, 'beautiful, inviting, welcoming'. In it are housed the children's officer (the Director of Child Welfare), the probation officers, the education officer, the youth welfare officers, the youth employment officers, the Moral Welfare Society, the NSPCC, the Adoption Society, the school care committee, the Invalid Children's Aid Association, the Family Welfare Association, the various national youth organisations, the Health Visitors, the Marriage Guidance Council, and perhaps even the Family Service Unit. And for good measure, 'I would like the Juvenile Court to hold its sessions there.'

The Times (28 April 1955) paid him the compliment of a leader. Basil's scheme, it said, was 'wholesale amalgamation' whereas what was wanted was co-ordination and 'a reduction of administrative separatism'.

Nine years after he had noted in his diary the merits of centralisation as he saw it in Australia the recommendations of the Ingleby Report (Cmd 1171 of 1960) called for a unified family service, and those of the Seebohm Committee (Cmd 3703 of 1968) for joint planning committees, with participation of the children authorities, the education and health committees, the probation and after-care services, and the police.

Another practice which he wanted the English courts to copy from Australia and New Zealand was the destruction of the record where a juvenile had been given an absolute or conditional discharge. Writing in 1956 he urged that if no further offence was committed within three or four years there should be no blot on the child's name, and he would have liked the same to be done in the case of adults. In 1974 rules in many ways similar were introduced in England by the Rehabilitation of Offenders Act, affecting adults as well as juveniles, for whom the 'rehabilitation period' was reduced.

In Australia the youth club movement included boys', girls' and mixed clubs, and was controlled by the National Fitness Council, a body which in Basil's view placed too little emphasis on the 'spiritual element' in fitness. Information kindly supplied by the Australian Government shows that this comment was well founded because of the limits imposed on the NFC by the National Fitness Act, 1941, but that over the years it has moved towards the encouragement of self-development through community recreation as a means to active mental as well as physical fitness. Basil, rooted in the NABC tradition and with a strong prejudice—it is fair to call it that, although he rationalised it—against mixed clubs, said:

The N.F.C. has so many organisations, about 38, affiliated to it that it is overwhelmed. What is wanted here is an NABC which does not get all mixed up with Guides and Girls Friendly Societies. Then there would be real training for Boys' Club Leadership and real development of Boys' Clubs instead of all this training for fitness in all the organisations. Besides which, fitness is too narrowly interpreted as physical fitness . . . Unless the N.F.C. can be made to think on broader terms than physical fitness there is little hope for a good development in Youth work. Williams [The Rt Hon. Sir Edward John Williams, PC, KCMG, British High Commissioner] said he would bear this in mind.

The phrase 'I let myself go' occurs every now and then in the diaries of the lecture tours. He let himself go on the subject of Castlemaine Reformatory though it was, in a sense, by request. He writes to the Premier of Victoria.

My dear Premier,
You most kindly asked me to send you a report of my impression of Castlemaine . . . You also asked me not to 'draw in my punches' . . . I will do as you suggest.
I thought that Castlemaine was the worst Reformatory I have ever visited and consider it should be closed immediately . . . The place is an old-fashioned prison . . . It is entirely unsuitable even as a penal institution because there are no facilities for games except a small yard.

Having set out its faults at length, he continued:

The purpose of Reformatory treatment is the training of character. This can only be achieved through trust and understanding and friendship.
There must be freedom to do wrong before a boy can be strong enough to resist temptations. For such treatment specially trained men with a flair for the work are needed. There will be many failures. Many will abscond. But through team games loyalty, unselfishness and uprightness may be learnt, and the boys become infected by contact with men of high character. Besides character training over a period of 18 months or 2 years or even longer, boys can be taught a trade.

In fact the building was subsequently demolished and that is ground for inferring that Basil's report was accepted and acted upon.

Of the Police Boys' Camp at Kurrayong he says:

> Every building, all the roads and clearing of the trees has been done voluntarily by the Police and the older boys in their spare time. The most thrilling thing was to see half a dozen huge, hefty police officers, in singlet and shorts, ragging with the kids as though they were their younger brothers . . . The discipline, behaviour and happiness was grand—and infectious . . . It is really one of the most marvellous places I have seen for boys and the whole tone was superb.

Of an interview with the Minister of Education:

> This is the most important thing I have done so far. He is a grand fellow, full of ideals. I got him to agree to let Hicks come to England to explain to the Home Office the whole of the brilliant work of the New South Wales Child Welfare Department and to see our Youth Clubs. At the same time I spoke frankly about the N.F.C. which I said was failing.

In New Zealand he met H who had been chosen to come to England for the Olympic Games as a hurdler.

> He is a delightful young teacher . . . I brought him back to the Hotel to talk to him about Clubs . . . The Club movement is about non-existent here. This is my scheme over which I am immensely excited. The NABC must get hold of H as soon as he reaches England. They must fire him with passion for Club work and I on my side will do what I can whilst I am here to get a position made for him as Club Organiser for the Islands. It would indeed be grand to train him to do the work in his own country.

Tour in the West Indies

Basil begins his diary by saying that it was his colleague, Mr John Watson, CBE (Chairman of the South East London Juvenile Court), who had been invited to make the tour and that it was only when he found himself unable to go that Basil was asked to take his place. Basil had been to Jamaica with Bunny on a banana boat. 'I had loved it and longed to go back. I felt in a way I belonged to Jamaica.'

In Jamaica Juvenile Courts were to be set up under the Juveniles Law and to work under a Juveniles Authority. The Law had been passed in 1948 but there had been too little money for building and equipment, and for the training of enough men and women to do probation work. Consequently Basil's main concern was to press for the implementation of the law and he characteristically urged them to be adventurous and trust to the enthusiasm of volunteers, rather than wait for enough professionals to be trained. He had a 35-minute interview with the Chief Justice, Sir Hector Hearne, of which he wrote: 'the busiest and most important day so far . . . The Principal Probation Officer has said that the scheme cannot be worked unless there are 27 fully trained Probation Officers. This is of course utterly impossible from the point of view of man-power and finance . . . I did my utmost to persuade the Chief Justice.' He then advised him to open the Juvenile Courts with two lay justices, using voluntary workers as probation officers, who would be trained by such professionals as they had available; above all they should proclaim the Juvenile Law throughout the Island.

Of a meeting with Premier Bustamente at the university he wrote:

> He came into the lecture but after 5 minutes he got up and took me out. 'It's you I want to listen to' he said, 'not all that theoretical stuff. Life's too short for that. I want to be practical and do something today; I may be gone tomorrow.' I had nearly half an hour's talk with him during which he sat silently with his eyes closed . . . When I had finished he said 'You have convinced me; the Law shall be proclaimed at once. I had opposed it up to now because it would have cost

too much. No one has ever shown me that it could be implemented without great expense until you came. Thank you, it shall be done.' I told him that now I could feel that 'my journey was really necessary' and we walked to the car with his hand on my shoulder. An extraordinary person but a very tired man.

As to their clubs he said, 'Some of the clubs here are of a very high standard, and very much better than many in England.' Of a boys' club he said, 'To my joy there is an attendance register and a penny a week is demanded . . . I was greatly impressed by the fact that it was broadly catering for the poorest type of child.'

Of a girls' club: 'The tone was excellent and I doubt whether there are many clubs affiliated to the NAGC which are as good as this one.'

Of 'Clubland' he said: 'This is one of the very best clubs I have *ever* seen. Like the R.C. club . . . it caters for the really under-privileged . . . I was so exhilarated by the spirit of this wonderful club that I was . . . able to address them from the depth of my heart. After which Adams [the Rev. D. V. Adams, Chairman of the Trinidad Youth Council] led us all in a short but moving prayer. A glorious experience.'

Basil thought that a practical demonstration of a Juvenile Court as run in England would be useful.

So we arranged the end of the room in Toynbee style. Martin Blake, of British Council, a native woman and I constituted the Bench, and although they only had ten minutes to rehearse it we tried 3 'cases' which were absolutely perfect in their delicious humour and satire and which demonstrated the brilliant histrionic powers of the Jamaican.

The first case was a 10 year old 'beyond control' boy. To take the part the biggest and fattest man had pulled his trousers above his knees, let his shirt hang out and had taken off his shoes and socks. All the time his 'mother', a pretty young dark girl, was giving evidence he kept on scratching his bottom and wiping his nose on the back of his hand.

After a description of the three cases he went on:

It was not only the delightful humour which kept one in
fits of laughter . . . it was the absurd resemblance to
London which absolutely thrilled me . . . and kept me in
fits of laughter. We had been a grand team of
fellow-workers, and this was our last session. I felt
impelled to ask them if they would allow me, a Jew and a
white man, to lead them in prayer. It was a wonderful
ending to a wonderful course.

On his last day in Jamaica he wrote:

Houghton [the Education Officer] said 'I wish you were
here to get this Juveniles Authority going.' I said 'I would
like to very much . . . my great-grandfather made a great
deal of money out of this people, which has enabled me to
live the life I have as a voluntary social worker and which
provided me with the best education in England. I would
like to give back to this people something of what they
have given me . . . I should love to come back to them . . .
How wonderful it would be if I were asked. Am I too old?
I can still run a boys' club. I can still dream dreams. I still
love my neighbour and these black and brown and yellow
neighbours are so very lovable, so very child-like. Am I too
old? I wonder.'

There are entries referring to a problem which the West
Indians dealt with better than he could. He was not the man to
affront his hosts by an unappreciative bearing towards rum
cocktails, at once the pride and profit of the islanders. 'We all
chose rum punch for our cocktail . . . at lunch I was fool
enough to have a whiskey and soda . . . I went through the
agony of trying to keep awake.'

At a luncheon party he was given 'an excellent green cocktail
of rum and absinthe' after which, in fluent Berner Street, he
admits to 'having got partly schnozzled'.

He submitted to the Government of Barbados a seven-page
report on the running of industrial schools, which was used by
the Advisory Board as a guide-line. Before he left that island on

his way home an official of the West Indian Development Board said to him, 'You lit a flame in Jamaica; you have done the same thing here.' On his return to England the British Council wrote to him: 'We still hear from all the Colonies you visited of the immense value of the work you did there, and it is most satisfying when concrete results of this kind follow so soon on your tour.'

12

Basil's Religion

Since religion was the dominating factor in Basil's life it might be well to take a closer look at that which he inherited and at the influences under which he formed his own and thus to see what the polemics were all about.

About 1840-1 a group of English Jews following the reformist movement which had developed in western Europe and America, seceded from the congregations built up after the Re-settlement in 1656 and founded the West London Synagogue of British Jews. In this synagogue, of which Basil's grandfather had been a president, his father brought him up.

The religion of the parent bodies was traditional Judaism, regulated in its practice by the Oral Law as it had developed over the centuries, which in turn derived its binding force from the belief in the Mosaic authorship of the Pentateuch. For the reformers, on the other hand, the validity of a religious observance had to be tested by the question, 'Does it minister to the religious life?' For the rest, they accepted the traditional belief in God and the feeling of being responsible to him, and they believed that the Old Testament contained, together with other matter and as far as it went, a revelation of God's will. They required an acceptance of the standards of morality and ethics which had been developed by the rabbis from Biblical origins, laying special emphasis as much in practice as in preaching on the traditional doctrine that to occupy oneself with social welfare ('good works', to use the Hebrew idiom) was a religious duty; 'it was to be the task of the reformist to explore ways of bringing the insights of religion to problems affecting society as a whole'.[1] Neither the Mosaic authorship of the Pentateuch nor the literal inspiration of the Bible nor the right to criticise its text were issues in the dispute which led to the secession.

The liturgy which gave expression to this change of outlook was based on the assumption that 'it becomes a congregation to adapt the ritual to the wants of its members'. Much of the traditional liturgy whether as prose or poetry was of great beauty; of some of the prayers it has been said 'their sublime simplicity makes one wonder whether the language of prayer has ever reached a higher plane'.[2] It was read in Hebrew and all of it was intoned; if there was a choir it was male, unaccompanied by any instrumental music. Men and women sat apart and heads had to be covered. A Sabbath morning service might take three hours, and the sermons were in Spanish and Portuguese. Parts of this service which seemed to the reformers 'deficient in devotional tendency' were removed and a few new prayers were composed, but in general it was 'altogether based on the existing ritual'. Yet before fifty years had passed, Basil's father, at the request of his rabbi, was submitting suggestions as to the causes of meagre attendance and general lack of enthusiasm.

David Henriques begins with a generalisation which today will surprise or console parents as the case may be.

'A revolutionary feeling', he says, 'exists everywhere between the younger generation and their seniors. Their great desire is to throw off all restraint and to govern themselves.' He goes on to say what is wrong. The service, which is in any case too long, is in Hebrew, which nobody understands; the sermons should be shorter and contain 'home truths which will help them (the young) in their daily life'. Two new hymns chosen by the younger members should be sung each week. Finally, there is a wistful mention of a reform which he thinks at least one or two members would support; it is that men and women should sit together.

About twenty-five years after David Henriques had made his plea for reform the conduct of the service had been changed in a way that reflected the English environment. A substantial proportion of the prayers were read in English, and where Hebrew was used chant or plain-song was discarded; an organ was played and men and women sat together in the congregation, and sang together in the choir. In the latest edition of their prayer book the compilers have sought 'to preserve the rich and hallowed values of the inherited Jewish ritual and . . . to meet the needs of the present age of modifying and omitting where this has been deemed advisable by re-introducing some ancient prayers and by adding others entirely new'.

But these changes were too late for Basil, and by the time he went up to Oxford the service had ceased to 'minister to his religious life'; he wanted something else. He was not very studious, so it is unlikely that he read the whole of the *Bible for Home Reading* when he began it at Harrow, and it was probably in his first term at Oxford that he read C.G.M.'s *Liberal Judaism*. Echoes of these two books recur throughout Basil's utterances.

The ideas that were cardinal to his religious thinking are to be found in *Liberal Judaism*, though he could not have denied—but would have been reluctant to concede—that similar beliefs with varying degrees of emphasis had always been inherent in the traditional teaching. 'The essence and validity of religion depend on the belief that there is a living and actual relationship between God and man.' 'The truly religious man is he who feels that God is near him, who feels the divine presence.'

In fact the feeling of communion with God was the whole of Basil's religion. Whenever he dealt with people as preacher, teacher, or counsellor, this was the sum of what he had to say. The purpose of prayer was to make this communion possible and to invite the action and influence of God on man: the purpose of beauty perceived through the senses, whether in nature or art, was to create an awareness of God.

Other ideas were less important but provided a useful framework in which he could make his religion work.

'The belief that Moses wrote the Pentateuch is not an essential doctrine and will gradually disappear.'

'The new Judaism does not believe . . . that the whole law is Mosaic, that the Law is eternally binding upon Jews and does not involve a belief in the divine origin or the permanent religious value of the dietary laws' (from *Liberal Judaism*).

Two other propositions which became fixed in his mind are to be found in the *Bible for Home Reading*. 'We are both

Englishmen and Jews.' 'The only true functions of the Jew are with God and goodness.' The mission of Judaism does not imply a restoration to Palestine, 'for the Jews are something other and higher than a nation. They are a religious brotherhood who hold together and remain apart not for political or national but for religious ends.' Basil accepted C.G.M.'s view that Judaism was a religion or nothing; neither nationality nor race could be accepted as a substitute. 'I have no bond with a Jew', he said, 'who denies the unity of God and the duty to love him with heart, soul and might.'

On the fly-leaf of *Fratres*, January 1946, he put a quotation from C.G.M.[3] 'Liberal Judaism believes in, and aims at, a universal Judaism, universal both in doctrine and in form. It holds that a national religion is an absurdity or at all events an anachronism.' When his founding of the Jewish Fellowship (see pp.115-19) is considered it must be remembered that not only did he hold this view with passionate sincerity, but that as recently as 1917 it could be reasonably called the view of Anglo-Jewry. A letter appeared in *The Times* of 17 May 1917 signed by D. L. Alexander, KC, the President of the Board of Deputies, and C.G.M., the President of the Anglo-Jewish Association, protesting 'strongly and earnestly' on the same grounds against the 'Zionist doctrine that all Jewish communities constituted one homeless nationality' for which a political centre and an always available homeland in Palestine were necessary. It would therefore be unjust to impute to him any other motive such as social or class prejudice. His character was robust enough to resist such ideas. So far from trying to merge his Jewishness with his environment by a kind of protective mimicry, he brandished it aloft whenever he was addressing non-Jews. On any matter even remotely affecting religion he would say, 'I am a Jew, I can only speak to you as a Jew; there must be no false pretences.'

Basil accepted what he had received but he could have argued little of it against a competent opponent; good friends of his, on both sides, warned him that some of his statements were facile, invalid, or over-simplified. He was, as we have seen, no theologian and he scarcely knew any Hebrew except what faithful Miss Prins[4] and Sam Kay (see p.176) had taught him to read. But it fitted in very well with the sort of religion which he wanted to profess himself and by which alone he hoped to lead and guide his clubs. It was not only the dietary laws. If there was no Mosaic origin for the Pentateuch the whole of the Law as formulated by the rabbis would, he would say, lose its binding force. Forms of 'work' prohibited on the Sabbath, the 'second days' of festivals, so many of the rules and practices which under the Berkeley Street dispensation had been at least capable of 'ministering to the religious life' could now, he thought, be taken out of the category of religious matters which a Jew need take into account.

Until he went to Oxford Basil had never encountered Jewish traditionalism, but as time went on he learnt more about it, and knew the 'short answers'—answers, that is to say, to questions that went not very far below the surface. After all, he had been the affectionate disciple of C.G.M., had walked and talked with Israel Brodie and had known Herbert Loewe for twenty-five years. Yet he could never enter into the feelings of one who professed and practised traditional Judaism. He paid it lip-service, yet it was honestly done, because he was not pretending but merely speaking within the limits of what he understood.

He seems never to have understood that traditional Judaism was a synthesis of religion and history in which a special part was assigned to human intelligence and reason, to all of which its liturgy gave expression. To him a synagogue was a Jewish church and not, as it had always been, a house of assembly or of learning; his concern with what he called 'decorum' reflects the influence of the college chapel rather than the frame of mind in which congregants assemble—to pray, certainly but primarily to enact the familiar and animated ritual of collective religious worship.

So far as his doctrine was that of Progressive Judaism it was bound to meet with the disapproval of the traditionals though many became his close friends and all of them respected his social work. An orthodox rabbi[5] wrote to him:

> With all your effort and good-will, your idealism and
> sincerity, you are travelling the wrong road. You are
> unwittingly selling the eternal Israel in order to achieve a
> temporary accommodation.

To which he answered:

I say that every man guided by the scholars and saints of the past and of the present, and by the communal conscience of the synagogue to which he belongs, must carry out those commandments which his conscience dictates.

Some of them, however, were antagonised and felt that they had reason to be affronted. He was avowedly carrying on a movement intended to spread Progressive Judaism in a district which had always been predominantly orthodox. Writing to Anthony de Rothschild before the Settlement was built he said: 'The most far-reaching work we are likely to do is the introduction of Progressive Judaism into the very heart of a superficially orthodox ghetto with its second generation of unorthodox young people.' In the 1930 preface to his Settlement Prayer book he prays that through his book the doctrines of Progressive Judaism may be more widely spread. Yet he could produce good reasons for refuting the charge of leading an attack on traditional Judaism. He could say that all his club members had full liberty of conscience as to the place and form of their worship and could add that when they came to him their minds had not received the impress of any effective religious faith. Here he was on strong ground. In 1906 the Annual Report of Hutchison House had stated: 'The Committee cannot but recognise that religious indifference and profound ignorance of the essential portions of their own faith are dominating features of East End youth.' In 1961 he was maintaining that most young Jews were so muddled by their religious education—'often perverted'—and the contrast presented by their parents' indifference that they could not possibly achieve the standard to which they ought to adhere.[6] On the other hand he seems to have forgotten about this spiritual vacuum when he addressed the Religious Weekly Press Group and said, 'The absence of delinquency and drunkenness among the Jews is due above all to the peculiarity of the place of religion in the Jewish home.' He could also say that his clubs and Settlement were kitchenwise strictly adapted for compliance with the dietary laws and that they were closed throughout the Sabbath except for the purpose of the

Synagogue. Nevertheless some of them felt that in dealing with evidence on which he based his opinions he was selective and biased. In considering the relationship between God and man C.G.M. had used the spatial metaphor 'inward, outward' or 'internal and external'. Basil, his opponents would have said, was a little facile in using the metaphor. He lumped together the whole of orthodox Jewish practice, comprising as it does law, custom, function and symbolism, in one comprehensive category which he called 'external ceremonies'. From such a premise specious or biased conclusions could easily follow.

In some quarters he gave the impression of polarising Jews into two groups: on the one hand, those who like him and his Progressives had a true or 'inward' faith and on the other the orthodox who were given over to 'ceremonies and externalities'. Of course there was always a saving clause for the 'sincere' who, even if unenlightened, must have their due. But it was felt that the grant of their due was a little grudging and perhaps a little condescending.

The United Synagogue was the largest and most important of the traditional groups and its President took off the gloves. He wrote:

> What makes you go so wrong is that you (and C.G.M.) persist in drawing a purely imaginary picture of traditional Judaism and then throwing stones at it. Our creed bears no sort of resemblance to your ugly picture . . . You should avoid the habit of telling us that we are liars and cowards and that you have the courage to say openly what we secretly believe and deliberately conceal . . . It is criminal
> that you should try and persuade people that they are Liberal Jews by telling the great bulk of Jews that their religion is incompatible with their patriotism. This is a calumny, dangerous only if spread broadcast . . . and the crime lies in using your money to distribute it broadcast to the ignorant multitude who do not know that what you state as facts are really imaginary pictures.

In fact, Basil was biased. As early as 1924 he had written to a friend, one of the lay leaders of the Anglo-Jewish community, saying that he was absolutely convinced that

Progressive Judaism was the only form of Judaism that could survive in this country. Such a conviction is not favourable to an impartial assessment of rival religious doctrine. Among Basil's papers were a number of letters from C.G.M. written, as far as can be guessed—the dating does not give the year—between 1910 and 1924, which show that they had the highest regard for each other and were very close friends. Basil called him 'my friend and master'. Many of the letters merely give news of common interest with a little light comment on people and current events. Others, taken together, amount to an epitomised critique of Basil's life as a religious 'activist'. They submitted scripts for each other's approval, and collaboration in tract-writing is suggested. He described an article of Basil's as 'noble, lucid and sincere' and a sermon as 'full of fire and intensity'. On the other hand he accused Basil of being unfair to both orthodox and Liberal Judaism in saying that he advocates neither and is preaching Judaism pure and simple. It is presumptuous to sweep away orthodoxy with a contemptuous gesture: 'Saintly and orthodox lives can go together . . . Your position is weak . . . I am not sure that your theology is sound.'

At the root of the master's love for his disciple was 'the experience of God' by which Basil said he was always sustained and moved, and which seems to have mattered more to C.G.M. than his doctrine. 'Give your doctrine no label, just live it and teach it.' Of Basil's sermon on God as shepherd he said: 'It is one of the most beautiful and noble things I have ever read . . . absolutely inspired, full of light, religion and experience . . . If it was I who ,"started" experience in you it makes me conceited.'

Let us now hear what Basil has to say on: the nature of God, Judaism, Progressive and Orthodox Judaism, Ceremonies, Synagogue services, Prayer, Religious education, Jewish nationalism.

On the Nature of God

We Jews believe that we have direct access to God without any mediation. He is the Creator of the Universe which he sustains by His own unalterable laws. He is perfect in His Goodness and the source of all righteousness. He is spirit. He has built man in His image and has endowed him with His own divinity, giving him the power to recognise His being and the freedom to obey His laws, which he has gradually revealed through the prophets and seers of all ages . . .

God is one. In spite of all the evil which is seen and felt there are no two influences, but only the one God who has so designed it that man shall in the end overcome evil, and to enable him to do this man has, as part of his whole personality, a spirit which is greater than either his physical or his mental self, and which is indeed a breath of the divine holiness. The purpose of prayer is to remember this spirit within him. There is the direct relationship between God and man.

(From an article in the *Sunday Times* on 'Worship'.)

God in his wisdom often achieves miracles; hardened sinners turn from their ways.

(From 'God revealed in social service', 7 August 1952.)

We proclaim God as King. We acknowledge His awful power, His greatness, and His might. But He is something much more to us than this. Besides His sublime greatness and His transcendent otherliness, He is also very near to each of us. He has implanted within us part of this very self. We have within ourselves His Holy Spirit . . . He influences and changes us. He strengthens and guides. We believe with all our heart and mind that He cares for us, that we matter to Him, what we are and what we do. God is my creator, but He is also my Father, my Shepherd, my Guardian, my Rock and above all my Redeemer, my Saviour.

(From a sermon preached on New Year at the Settlement.)

If then, the Father is so near to us that He is within our very hearts there must be a very close connection between Him and us. We cannot see Him but we can feel Him. Whenever we think of Him we know that he is there and this feeling is what is called communion.

('The Kingdom of God', sermon on Penitential Sabbath 1915 at East London Synagogue.)

I cannot prove God to you; I know, I feel, I believe that He is. I cannot prove to you the rose smells sweet . . . I know, I believe, I feel these things.

(From a sermon preached on the 1st day of New Year, 1937.)

The God worshipped by the Jews is the Creator of the world . . . whose complete being will never be wholly comprehended, for, as our ancestors believed thousands of years ago, so would we today uphold, that no man can see God and live.

(From an article in the *Sunday Times* on 'Worship'.)

Like all created things in nature man's spirit grows and eventually withers away on its own, or as some of us would prefer to say through the care of God the creator.

(Lecture, 'The club with a purpose'.)

'God is' must mean something real to us. It must signify that although we cannot describe Him there is nevertheless a spirit which has existed and will exist for all time, who created the world and all that is therein and who still maintains the world which He created. The mere belief that 'God is' is not sufficient. We must also believe that the world and we who are within it are dependent upon Him, and that He continues to re-create us, to watch over us and to sustain us . . .

The moral law, which, I think, all theists maintain . . . is an external law.

The moral law . . . is an external law . . . revealed to man by God through His prophets, the inspired seers speaking in His name . . .

This external law never becomes wholly his own law because not only is its source God who is outside him, but also because he is always straining to obey a yet higher law, towards an ideal which is ever receding.

(Lecture on 'Discipline and Democracy'.)

On Judaism

The religious sense is the only sense in which I understand Judaism. Humanism is not Judaism, nor are agnostics Jews.

The election of the Jews is still a reality and the Jewish mission is still that the Jews shall be the servants of the Lord wherever they may be.

(From a sermon on the death of C.G.M.)

A Jew who apostasises for secular reasons is betraying his God and betraying his people.

(Article in *South of the Thames Jewish Society* on 'Mixed Marriages'.)

The core of Judaism is the ethical laws. They are enunciated with the divine sanction of 'I am the Lord' and because 'I, the Lord, command them' they must be obeyed, for 'ye shall fear God' which means stand in awe and reverence of Him, and therefore lovingly and willingly carry out all His instructions.

(From the *Fratres Anthology*.)

If Israel denies his God Israel must quickly perish. The twelve million Jews scattered about the world could not survive without the synagogue.

(Sermon on New Year, 1937.)

If, then, we are seeking to rebuild the waste places we can only be sure of success if they are built on the solid changeless foundations of Judaism. In order to do this Judaism must be the inspiration of our own personal lives, in the eradication of what is evil, and in the building up and spreading far and wide of all that is good . . . Thus since so much of our [Jewish Social Workers'] work depends on the interplay of our personality upon those with whom we work, Judaism must all the time be the source and well-spring of our lives.

('The spirit of service', Address to Conference of Jewish Social Workers, 1949.)

Progressive and Orthodox Judaism

I thought this morning that the remarks were too sweeping about the 'pots and pans religion of the home'. It may be a religion of pots and pans, but they are very much loved pots and pans. The truly Orthodox—and there are a good many of them—truly love their religion and they are sincere. Their ways may not be our ways but nevertheless they have set an example of sincerity, something real, something done for the sake of God, which I am afraid we do not find in what I may describe as 'unorthodox' homes.

The piety of the Orthodox Jew is recognisable to the world and his fellow Jews by the outward rites and ceremonies which he performs in the name of his religion. We, who have discarded so many Jewish rites and ceremonies, cannot be so recognised, but our piety can be known by our lives, by our humility, our justice, our loving kindness, our helpfulness, our pity, our love.

(Sermon on New Year, 1930.)

When this synagogue was founded we set out to prove that our interpretation of Judaism is the real and true interpretation of Judaism, the proper and right carrying forward of that traditional Judaism which has been progressive throughout the ages and which has always been adaptable to the aspirations of the Jews of its time. We set out to prove that religion and above all Judaism can be a real and living force in the lives of men today.

(Sermon on New Year, 1930.)

If we break the Sabbath and we do it believing it to be wrong then we ought to 'chuck' being club managers at once. If, on the other hand, we break the Sabbath according to orthodox rules and we do not think we are doing wrong by so doing then surely we can make our boys and girls see things from the same point of view as ourselves. The tragedy of the whole thing is that the average boy or girl breaks the Sabbath because it is too difficult, or too much trouble, or because they do not care. Perhaps I might put it this way: if we keep the Sabbath in a liberal way, let us teach the boys and girls our liberal point of view, and, if we are orthodox, from the orthodox point of view.

There can only be two kinds of Judaism, either Orthodox Judaism based upon a revealed religion, the adherents of which are bound by an outward immutable law, towards which they can allow their reason and their conscience to play no part, or Progressive Judaism based upon progressive revelation, the adherents of which are bound by a law which is written on the heart of every individual, which alone is free, within limitations, to expand, to discard and to modernise.

I have lived long enough among what is called the most orthodox Jewish community in this country to be able to say positively that Orthodox Judaism is dead for the vast majority of Jews today. Yet these English Jews are craving for an expression of their spiritual aspirations as they never have before. Progressive Judaism alone can satisfy it.

Our synagogue is unique in that it is affiliated to the Reform Synagogues in Britain as well as to the Liberal Synagogues. As the only Progressive synagogue in East London we have a special duty to spread in this area a knowledge of Progressive Judaism to that greatly increasing number of men and women who are dissatisfied with the other forms of service and with the principles on which they are based.

(Sermon on the progress of the Settlement, 28 April 1956.)

It is easy to understand the point of view of the truly Orthodox. He is at least consistent. His very intolerance is forgivable. He lives in a world apart, unaffected by scientific progress. His life consists in studying the various Rabbinic interpretations of the law, and in trying to fulfil its multifarious injunctions. He does not question, he obeys. It is not for him to doubt; he must submit. The carrying out of the law is not for him a burden, no matter how difficult it may be; it is always to him a peculiar joy to be able to obey the will of God.

There are not many truly Orthodox Jews in this country, and I am not concerned with them, but only with those so-called Orthodox Jews, who do not study the Talmud and who have probably done very little studying at all, but who carry on a traditional Judaism which has probably been orally transmitted to them from generation to generation.

Almost, if not quite the most important of all these traditions is to them the dietary law.

(Unidentified typescript.)

Because we have broken away from much that is practised and beloved by modern Orthodox Jews we have done so deliberately without apology. We hold the view which we have

146

because we are positive that we are right and they are wrong. It is we and not they who are the real successors of the Judaism of the Prophets. It is we who are developing along the right Jewish lines and not they, who are not developing at all. It is because it is we who are right and not they that with us lies the future of Judaism and Israel.

(New Year Sermons, 1930.)

On Ceremonies

We are never tired of speaking and thinking of the outward ceremonies of religion. For instance, surely you must have noticed even if you have not done it yourselves, how a group of young men and women will spend many hours of the time they devote to religious thought, in discussing whether it is really part of a day's work to carry a handkerchief upon the Sabbath. With all seriousness and sincerity, they will argue whether to do this is a greater sin against God than to poke the fire, or shave the beard or eat milk and meat together. But how often will they speak with one another of the deeper truths of religion? I mean, how much time do we spend in asking ourselves whether an unkind thought is a greater sin against God than an unkind action . . .

('Kingdom of God', sermon at East London, 1915.)

On Services

It is possible to have a combination of the old and the new; of the familiar and the unfamiliar, and this would seem to be the best form of service. Beloved airs and beloved words can give great comfort and revive precious memories. The new and unexpected retain the interest and keep the worshipper awake, both to his modern duties and his modern needs.

(Sermon at Special Service at Settlement Synagogue, August 1941.)

There is no doubt that the ceremonial of home life has helped more than anything else in the survival of Judaism throughout the ages. It has become economically almost impossible to keep the Sabbath in the traditional manner outside the ghetto. The intensification of the importance of Friday night on the one hand and on the other a broader interpretation of what is sacred and profane and of what is relaxation and what is labour, and of what is permissible and what not in order to keep the day holy, peaceful and restful should result in no loss of the Sabbath, and in no necessary segregation from one's neighbour.

('Relationship between Jews and Christians', Society of Christians and Jews, 1938.)

On Prayer

The purpose of prayer is to remember the spirit of God within us. There is the direct relationship between man and God . . .

We pray for others because we confide the secret longings of our heart to a loving Friend who knows our secret thoughts before we even utter them . . . We may even ask Him to perform miracles because we so urgently want them to happen. It is in order to confess these yearnings to Him who understands them rather than to try and make God change the laws by which he is completely bound.

(From an article in the *Sunday Times*.)

'Help me to alter the things that can be altered and to accept those that cannot, and above all give me the knowledge to decide the difference'. In that short message the author has summarised the very essence of religious philosophy.

(Sermon on 'Acceptance of God's will'.)

Club prayers are the fountain-head and source of the whole spirit of the club.

(From 'The place of religion in clubs', a lecture to the Association for Jewish Youth, 1931.)

Our thoughts are transferred to our fellow-creatures through some incomprehensible telepathy, and they may be upheld in a way we do not understand. The sufferer may be helped to bear his pain, the surgeon may unknowingly be given confidence . . .

the unjust and the cruel may be influenced by our petitions on their victims' behalf.

(From an article in the *Sunday Times* on 'Worship'.)

That confession of our day's work, that diary or record of our successes, failures, conquered temptations and lost ideals, which night by night we whisper to God.

(From an address given to the Oxford and St George's Club and the Oxford and Bermondsey Mission at 125 Cannon Street Road in 1915.)

On Religious Education

In the East End of London the ordinary chevras that spring up like mushrooms all over the place do not aim, and do not pretend to set out to have an influence over their boys and girls. They do not try to understand their outlook. Their rabbis are often extremely foreign and work in exactly the opposite direction to the clubs . . . I do not think one can want anything better in the way of religious education than that which is provided in the schools of the Jewish Religious Education Board . . .

At the age of thirteen the Jewish boy is sick to death of religious education. He is sick of the whole thing because he has never learnt to love his religion. He has had too much of it before he is old enough to appreciate it. The very thought of religion, as he grows up to manhood, becomes to him something that is not beautiful, not inspiring, not lovable, something that fills him with nothing but unhappy memories. The Jewish boy at thirteen is a boy who has the 'rim' of Judaism but not the 'hub'—the centre of his religion has been left out of his education—God as a Personal Father, God as the Master, God as the Spirit of Righteousness demanding righteousness, God as one to be feared in default of righteousness. Such a conception of God is absolutely foreign to the average boy who has only had the Talmud Torah, Cheder[7] or 'private rabbi education'. We find as they come into our clubs, our brigades and our scout movement, that they have lost that which I cannot help thinking (whether it is felt consciously or sub-consciously) is the most precious, the most wonderful thing in life, the knowledge of God's nearness, God's watchfulness, God's care for each individual being.

(From 'The place of religion in clubs'.)

I am sick of hearing so much of the God of Abraham, Isaac and Jacob. Let's hear more about our God.

(From 'The place of religion in clubs'.)

You cannot teach faith. Faith has got to be caught . . . The club leader's job is not to pour religion into them but to live a religious life so that the boys themselves wonder and admire and accept the faith which ennobles a good leader of a club to do the good things that he does do.

(Lecture on boys' clubs at Hounslow, 15 September 1956.)

I believe that the very foundations of a good life are based on the knowledge that a religion demands righteousness and that through religion adults and children alike are helped to attain it. That is the most important of all things and it must be taught in the home, in the school and in the club.

('I speak for myself', BBC London calling Asia, 29 September 1951.)

The leaders must become conscious that they are training boys and girls to become (a) labourers in the establishment of the Kingdom of God on earth, and (b) witnesses to the Gentiles of the righteousness of God, and they must always be instilling into members a consciousness of their responsibilities as members of the Chosen People, and that the unrighteousness of a Jew is a greater sin because he is the chosen agent of God.

('The work of the Religious Advisory Committee of the Association for Jewish Youth'.)

On Jewish Nationalism

He [C.G.M.] had a real dread that in a Jewish state Jews would feel themselves Jews by nationality and not by religion, and that nationality would take the place of religion in the heart of the Jew.

The fact that we have left religion out of our clubs has resulted in—I am trying to choose my words most carefully—what is to me the most objectionable type of Jew, that is the Jewish nationalist who has not got a religion behind him.

(From 'The place of religion in clubs'.)

There emerges the picture of a man who tells us that he feels within his soul the presence of God. Nothing could be more explicit than his prayer 'For Understanding':

'Lord of the Universe, I know not what Thou art and yet I feel Thy presence to be before me at all times.

Thou hast no eyes, and yet I know that no act or thought of mine is hidden from Thy sight; Thou hast no hands, and yet when I am faint and weak, I feel Thy love upholding me; Though hast not ears, and yet when I call unto Thee I know that Thou art listening; Thou hast no voice, and yet when I pray to Thee I hear Thy answer in my heart; Thou hast no form, and yet, O King, I see Thee ever before me.'

That was his own personal message, his gospel by which he hoped to put spiritual health within the reach of his clubs and his congregation; their response shows that he achieved his purpose.

13

Turning Point

At the end of the war Bunny arranged with trusted Settlement friends to take her place at home while she went to Germany with the Jewish Relief Unit. She was well qualified for such work. She had made herself fluent in German and she had learnt in Stepney something of the mind and speech of the Jewish refugee. She was in Germany for about six months and worked as director of a field unit.

When she came back she found Basil in a strange mood, as if slightly bewildered. His boys had changed. To some of the evacuated children he was only a remote figure. Others had married; their love and friendship remained but they were no longer dependent on him. With the new outlook on the relationship between the sexes, and all that it meant to his ideas about the purposes and management of a boys' club, he would never have been at ease. He was now in his fifty-sixth year. 'I am too old', he said, 'to tackle these post-war boys; they need someone younger who will handle them better.' The population of Stepney, too, was changing, and many of the old residents would not return. Some struck new roots in the countryside to which they had been evacuated; others, whose houses had been destroyed, were re-settled elsewhere. Newcomers to Stepney greatly reduced the proportion of Jews to non-Jews.

Above all, the Butler Education Act had changed the basis of youth work. It empowered the local authority to provide 'leisure-time occupation' by way of 'organised cultural training and recreative activities'. If the ratepayer was to give the money and pay the worker, was there still a place for such workers as he and such givers as Bernhard Baron? In 1947 the Stepney

Borough Youth Committee on which Basil had sat since the early days of the Club outlined its plans for community centres and youth organisations. Every area was to re-group its present facilities and have a 'neighbourhood unit'; but there was to be no interference with the interest which Church and Synagogue had long held in youth work. Basil said that he could not believe that the new youth centres would have the amazing spirit of friendship and loyalty to an ideal which characterised voluntary groups; it had not happened so far, he said, in any of the centres which were being run by local authorities or where the leadership was merely professional and vocational: 'If we are going to lose that spirit and the club atmosphere which binds the boys and girls together then for heaven's sake leave that work to the voluntary bodies and let your evening institutes and county colleges do the things which the voluntary organisations can't do. I am keen not to kill the voluntary movements but I am much afraid there's a real danger of that happening.'

In fact the country was on the threshold of the Welfare State and Basil was not alone in his bewilderment.

Furthermore, he was tired. Bunny wrote:

> He felt that the continued heavy burden of the
> administration of the Settlement was becoming more than
> he could continue to bear . . . It entailed in addition to
> fund-raising constant contact with residents and students to
> be trained . . . The strain of the war had sapped a good deal
> of his physical energy and he longed for an honourable
> respite from his ceaseless responsibilities . . . he wanted to
> write books and study problems of delinquency and
> religious activity . . . But he did not want to give up his
> contact with the boys and the Old Boys . . . He was
> becoming desperate with fatigue.

He told his sponsors that he wanted to resign but it was difficult, and looked like being impossible, to find someone whom he could train to take his place. Poor Basil, after all those exhortations to undergraduates, to school-leavers, to so many boys in so many clubs! It was the end of the war, the second of the two wars to end war, and society was everywhere responding to the universal need for re-construction and to the call of new careers opened up by advances in applied science, as if to justify the saying that all the noble arts of peace are dependent on war. Many, too, of the very people from whom Basil would have most liked to pick his successor were applying their altruism in voluntary service overseas.

Yet his luck held. His nephew Lionel Henriques visited the Settlement on his way back from the Fourteenth Army in Burma to his Rhodesian tobacco farm. There was much mutual affection and goodwill, and he agreed to be trained for the work provided he could arrange for the proper management of his farm. He joined the Settlement for training early in 1947. Basil's pleasure at the prospect of release and of being able to accept an invitation to go on a lecture tour in Australia was so mixed with self-reproach for having, as he thought, betrayed his trust that he fell into a state of dejection which made life difficult for his apprentice. Bunny wrote, 'Lionel was very patient and I shall always be grateful to him for this. He was anxious to begin and we set a date, 10 October, 1947, for him to start his new undertaking, for he knew the Settlement routine well by this time.'

So it came about that Basil and Bunny resigned on that date and Lionel Henriques took over.[1]

In the next Birthday Honours Basil's name appears as a CBE, 'lately Warden of the Bernhard Baron Oxford and St. George's Settlement; member of the council of the National Association of Boys' Clubs'.

14

Happy Warrior

'We have retired', said Basil, 'after thirty-three years of happiness.' Six years later he was telling an audience, 'I doubt whether there is anyone in this room who has had so much happiness or to whom life has been so good as it has been to me over the last forty-three years.'

His work, of course, was his happiness and he was to go on with it for another thirteen years.

He told Bunny when he retired that he wanted to write. He had already written *Club Leadership* in 1933 and *Indiscretions of a Warden* in 1937; these were followed by the *Fratres Anthology* and *Indiscretions of a Magistrate* both in 1950, *Club Leadership To-day* in 1951 and *The Home-Menders or the Prevention of Unhappiness in Children* in 1955.

Of his books *Club Leadership To-day* is perhaps the most important because in it Basil came to terms with the Butler Education Act and all that it implied for youth work. He conceded that very great benefit accrues to the youth centres from the supply of instructors for non-vocational activities such as hobbies. As to the 'club spirit' it can exist, he said, in a LEA youth centre but not in a Recreational Institution. Even in a youth centre it would gain very much by having voluntary managers both to create it and to keep it alive; 'You cannot pay a man to love his neighbour.'

This 'club spirit' which he was forever holding out as the very essence, the indispensable property, of a good club seems to be something indefinable, imponderable, such as to provoke sceptical comment. In his day the expression 'esprit de corps' was much used for what he calls a 'sense of belonging'; at least he used 'sense of belonging' when he seems to be referring to the 'club spirit' (see pp.57-8, 64). Is that what it meant? Or was it to be found in a club whose members were visibly filled with his own ardour and energy as well as his determination to be guided in everything they did by the will of God and, if so, was it just his own personal yardstick by which he would measure and judge a club? In his diary of his tour in Sweden (1949) he told how he was taken to some state-run clubs: 'There was no spirit, but the boys seemed to like just the sort of things that English boys like . . . No leadership, no spirit. They have no idea how to create the club spirit . . . God save us from L.E.A. clubs.' Could he possibly tell after watching a few games, or was he merely giving rein to his prejudices? Whatever the answer, the observations of two very knowledgeable and impartial judges are relevant. C.B. Russell's widow, in her revised edition of his *Lads' Clubs*, has this to say of Basil's club: 'Any observant visitor must note within the first five minutes the blithe, energetic spirit which prevails'; in the same book she quotes from an address given by the Warden of Brighton Boys' Club: 'It is quite likely that there is a "spiritual wind" which blows round a billiard table . . . or it may hover round a boxing ring.'

The deep conviction and high moral standard of the ethical and religious prescriptions for a good club as they appear in *Club Leadership* are clear. Yet they are counsels of perfection, and some will say that they may discourage recruitment because they call for talents which not all club leaders can be expected to possess. In 1959, giving evidence to the Albemarle Committee on the prevention of delinquency he suggested the interchangeability of club leaders and probation officers.

When he is writing about the practical requirements of a club, its constitution, rules, structure and equipment he is at his very best. He speaks with the obvious authority of a master of the whole machinery of club and camp life in all its details.

His books had to be written in his spare time, and he was still doing everything (except being warden of a settlement) of which an account has been given in 'The Day's Work'. Besides this he was now an 'authority' on juvenile delinquency, and indeed on youth in general, its morals, manners and upbringing. Invitations to speak poured in from all over the country. Not only did he refuse very few but he insisted that the list of those which he felt a duty to accept should be comprehensive. So we find him talking for example to the Consett Ladies' Tea Club in Durham, or the Wimbledon Guild of Social Welfare as well as taking part in a series on 'Justice' arranged by the Warden of All Souls or addressing a meeting of magistrates in Manchester or giving an important lecture in Birmingham. About thirty-five such occasions a year, often with a day's journey before and after, were a burden. During most of this time he was fighting but not complaining against ill-health. In 1951 glaucoma set in and by 1955 he had lost the sight of one eye. 'So far my other eye has not been affected so I can carry on with my work. That's all that matters; there is still so much to be done here', he told a reporter. Next year he was so tired that Bunny took him for a holiday to Corsica but when he came home he had to have an operation for cancer.

After the operation he asked the surgeon, 'Is it cancer?' 'Yes, it is', was the reply, 'but you'll be all right; I've left you enough stomach to carry on your ordinary life.' Whereupon Basil thanked him, shut his eyes and slept soundly. During his convalescence in Surrey he wrote the pamphlet, 'The Faith of a Jew' and then went off with Bunny on a health-seeking tour to South Africa from which he returned able, as his surgeon had said, to carry on his ordinary life. Yet he became ill through overwork in 1958 and a year later his heart became affected.

In January 1955 he received a Knighthood and in September of that year became time-expired and retired from the East London Juvenile Court, on which he had served for thirty years. Although he continued to be on the panel of justices at Bow Street Magistrates' Court and at Quarter Sessions, he was free to go on another lecture tour to America. He sailed on the *Queen Mary* and thoroughly enjoyed it. 'I cannot get over the gorgeous sumptuousness and luxury of this amazing ship . . . It quite saddens me not to be able to use all the towels each day. If I wipe my hands on one it is replaced almost immediately by a clean one.'

A fellow-passenger was the Duke of Windsor. Basil wrote:

On the captain's advice I had written to H.R.H. reminding him of his visit to Betts Street, of the Albert Hall Meeting, and of his inspection of Basil House and saying that should he desire to see me I am at his service . . . I got a telephone message to say that he would like me to meet him in the smoking room. He talked to me alone there for three quarters of an hour. He was in excellent form . . . He said how pleased he was that I had contacted him, and I certainly enjoyed my talk with him.

In 1961 his heart condition became worse. He was still doing his full day's work; in the latter part of the year he was conducting two of his very exacting 'campaigns'. But he was getting weaker. Bunny drove him about wherever she could; where she could not, he found it difficult to walk. He went to Cambridge to address the World Conference of Faiths dreading the length of the Cambridge platform. On 10 November he came back from a lecture in a state of collapse and went to hospital next day. He was growing weaker but was able to see a few of his family and intimate friends. He dictated letters to Bunny resigning from presidencies and chairmanships.

He died on 2 December with Bunny at his bedside. She writes, 'Basil lay quietly and I sat by him. After some time he moved his hand away from mine and I knew he was making his peace with God; his gaze was elsewhere; his face was serene because he was unafraid.'

15

Retrospect

Basil's Knighthood was expressed to be 'for services to youth welfare'. Perhaps it is now time to try to assess them.

It is too much to say that he solved any problems or initiated any measures. His claim to be mentioned in an account of the social services of his age would rest on the qualities which he brought to them. He was, as Mr John Watson has said, a born reformer. It was his luck to be entering on his career at the beginning of 'a period of steady and purposeful advance'.[1] It was his merit that he was always found to be in the forefront of that advance and to be adding the considerable power of his personality to its momentum.

He was forward-looking. He accepted whole-heartedly the new teaching that in dealing with juvenile offenders society's paramount duty was to reclaim and reform and to punish only when punishment served those purposes. Writing to a friend about probation he said, 'If only we could make a real success of this non-institutional training for the minor types of delinquents one can almost dream of the day when for more serious delinquents probation with very strict conditions will take the place of prison, the worse the offender and the more serious the crime the stricter to be the conditions of probation.'

He regarded the preventive side as far and away the most important, and prevention meant education. He feared the effects of the unoccupied mind and the unsatisfied craving for adventure. At the age of thirty-three he was in the thick of the campaign for compulsory schooling up to fifteen; at sixty he was baiting the hook of reclamation with good juvenile story-books for juvenile probationers; after his death he was quoted in the House of Commons as the magistrate who said that where there were adequate playgrounds there was always less youthful crime. He seemed to be trying to realise the ideal which he had so passionately put before his parents when he was at Oxford, 'to give away to others, who have not, all that wealth and education have given me'.

He set himself to learn something of the current psychological approach to crime and to put what he had learnt into practice. Sin, he said, was a complex; he saw delinquents as 'mentally sick' and his task as diagnosis and prescription. His articles on the subject provoked controversy. Writing to him in 1947 his friend Sir Leo Page, a noted criminologist, said:

> I think your article is quite beautiful—none of that narrow bigotry which comes of being tied to actual facts! . . . In 1939 there were 2000 boys sentenced to Borstal, in 1946 there were 3000 and there should have been 5000 . . . But don't go too far. You will do harm if, with the influence due to your grand social work, you lead plain folk to neglect the dreadful depravity of young offenders today . . . You have no right to be blind to facts.

Yet he could not altogether discard his inherited concepts of sin and moral turpitude, nor substitute for such terms euphemisms, however scientific, such as 'deviation' and 'anti-social conduct'; in a proper case punishment would be part of the prescription, though he had his own ideas about its value and purpose.

In a report on 'Boy Prisoners' which he wrote in 1937 he said:

> Prison as a deterrent utterly and completely fails in its purpose . . . A short sentence in a place of detention may be desirable so long as it is followed by supervision by a probation officer. Such places must not be called prisons, even if the life in them resembles that of prison life. No one under the age of 21 must know what a prison sentence is.

In 1958 the increase in crime among the 17–20 age group moved him to compare them with their parents.[2]

Psychologically they are the same, rebelling against authority, inquisitive, effervescing with an exuberance of high spirits, willing to meet a challenge for good or bad, wanting to meet together with others of the same age and life interest, forming either into anti-social gangs or into teams working for the good of society.

Section 1 of the Sexual Offences Act 1967 would have elicited the following:

It is no more a sin for a man to have homosexual desires than it is for him to have heterosexual desires. He sins when he gives expression to his desires, and he commits a crime when he does so with the young. It will always be a sin to have a sex relationship with a consenting adult over the age of 21. Should it cease to be a crime to have it in private? . . . Until the state reaches the height of condemning the evils of fornication and adultery as a crime against the welfare of its citizens there is no logical reason for treating homosexual indulgence differently (from an article in *Time and Tide*).

For men who had committed 'abominable crimes' of violence he favoured very long sentences of detention which might be a deterrent and would in any case protect the public and provide an opportunity for reformation. He opposed corporal punishment for men and boys (letter to *The Times*, 9 March 1950).

Speaking to a gathering of probation officers at Caxton Hall he stated five objects of his Juvenile Court. Basil is recognisable by the parentheses.

1 To protect the public.
2 (not necessarily in order of importance) The reformation of the defendant.
3 Deterrence.
4 An attempt to bring home to the defendants that they have wronged somebody and must make amends.
5 (and of tremendous importance) To bring home to the parents their responsibility for their children.

The machinery for carrying out these intentions had been created by a series of Childrens Acts beginning in 1908, which had established juvenile courts, the probation service, and a number of custodial establishments where the work of reformation could at least be attempted. It was the task of civil servants, magistrates and, indeed, of all who cared deeply for good citizenship, to be constantly testing these components, discovering defects and devising remedies. No one entered on this task more ardently than Basil. On the Bench he inspired the court probation officers with confidence in the new doctrine so that they in turn gave him the information and advice which he needed for his 'prescriptions'. Out of court he worked in committee with his fellow magistrates and with the Home Office; he visited remand homes and approved schools, corresponded with their headmasters, and followed up individual cases sent by him into the care of the local authority.

His chosen objectives in this field seem to be those of one who had lived for years among juveniles as their friend and guide and knew their reactions. So we find him fighting against 'contamination' in remand homes—he had seen it happening in St George's—and insisting on the necessity of after-care because it meant more friendship and more guidance. He complained, perhaps too much, of what he called the 'upheavals' when the juveniles leave one place of custody for another and called for 'Observation centres' instead of proceeding by trial and error. There should, he said, be a really qualified psychologist in every approved school.

Perhaps he was too forward-looking. He was apt to concern himself more with the end than the means. Wherever he worked, whether among prisoners, or the sick, or the poor, or the young, he was moved by a desire to alleviate hardship and redress injustice. Others, no less moved, who may have gone more patiently and carefully—perhaps more objectively—into the question of ways and means, had a clearer understanding of the difficulties: too little money to build, too few nurses for the hospitals, probation officers for the courts, welfare workers for after-care, so that it might be better to change one's ground or be content with half a loaf. It was hard for Basil to do either without showing resentment and lashing out at the nearest administrator.

He was a man in whom courage and compassion combined to form the mainspring of his character. He had proved himself a brave soldier; the moral courage which he showed in peace was perhaps a little easier for one who like Basil had to look to no one for his living. Yet he never shrank from a course of action for fear of obloquy, or ridicule or merely isolation. He could say what he liked and said it.

His time at Toynbee Hall, short as it was, must have been somehow formative; up to 1911 its secretary had been C. R. Attlee and its warden Maurice Birley. In such an environment he must have learnt in what channels the 'tide of social pity' was likely to flow. Yet nothing indicates more clearly the style in which his life's work was going to be done than his reason for leaving Toynbee. He gives it in *Indiscretions of a Warden*. 'Except that I thoroughly enjoyed working with Robin Montefiore . . . I was not happy at Toynbee . . . I suppose I never got the hang of the place. Everyone seemed so fearfully sociological . . . I was worried to know how out of place it would have been to invite club boys to one's room or to supper with the residents as had been the Bermondsey custom.' It was not merely that he was not an academic, though his understanding was able, quick and resourceful. He knew very well that his part in social service was to be played through the impact of his personality on his fellow-men, as it was to be throughout his life, in his Club, on the Bench, on the platform or in the pulpit. He was impatient to begin.

These qualities of heart and mind were enhanced by his presence. A writer in the *Observer* said of him, 'His extraordinary height and striking good looks would make him conspicuous anywhere but he stands out primarily as one of the really good men of our age.'

He had a manner, too. *The Times* obituary on Harold Llewellyn Smith, headmaster and boys' club leader, has this passage: 'Harold soon fell under the spell (there is no other word) of Basil Henriques.' Harold introduced him to his father, Sir Hubert Llewellyn Smith, GCB, the great civil servant, who was in turn lured by him into the boys' club movement, and became chairman of the NABC. Years later he wrote to Basil telling him of the many friends he had made in the movement: 'but there is no one in it whom I look on with greater affection than yourself'.

Did he know of the spell? There is a story not quite on that level about a niece, an undergraduate, whom he took out to luncheon and who said, when he tried to lure her into similar paths, 'Uncle Basil, it's no use turning on the charm.'

He was a persuasive speaker. He had a flair for the value of antithesis, metaphor and simile, which made him a good pamphleteer and, coupled with a useful working knowledge of the Bible, enabled him to keep the average level of his immense output of sermons well above mediocrity and on occasion to raise it to a high degree of eloquence and power. Yet these qualities, combined with his exuberance of language, made him prone to the faults and distortions of a propagandist. He sometimes appeared more concerned with the power of his words to convey his message than with their strict correspondence with logic or with the facts of the case.

He had begun by building a club which was not only of the highest standard in point of membership and achievement but was also by common acclaim an example of the 'threefold fitness of body, mind and spirit' which the founders of the National Association held out as the true purpose of their boys' clubs. For twenty years he travelled around Britain carrying that message to his countrymen with unsurpassed forcefulness and fervour.

When he first set out to live among the boys of St George's he declared that his purpose was to serve God by serving mankind. Looking back on it he said, 'It has meant the unconscious sharing of myself—my ideals, my interests, my religion—with others whose burdens I have also attempted to share.' When he had finished his work it was said of him by one of his closest colleagues[3] that of those who strove for the happiness of the youth of his age he was 'among the noblest of the giants'.

16

R. L. H.

If I had a duty to add to the portrait of Basil a sketch of Bunny, I have backed out of it, contributing only some facts within my own knowledge and giving place to those who can make value-judgments without the bias of blood-relationship. I have therefore asked three people who knew and worked with Bunny for very many years to let me use their assessments and thus make it a composite chapter. They are (in order of appearance) Lily Caminer (L.C.), widow of David Caminer; Charles Dreyfus (C.D.) who had served the Settlement as club manager, joint treasurer and chairman of its executive committee, and my wife (A.G.L.) who knew Bunny before she knew me.

R.L.H.

'Can you imagine someone good looking, pretty features, curly dark hair, fairly tall, slender, clever, imaginative and talented in many directions?' That was what Lily Caminer thought when Bunny started her Girls' Club in 1915. Writing of her in her old age Charles Dreyfus says, 'Those who only knew her as an old lady, bent, with bad eyes and swollen legs, would have difficulty in picturing her some fifty years earlier in her ballet dress, teaching the elements of ballet to the girls in the club.'

Rose Louise Loewe was born on 17 August 1889 in Stoke Newington, the only daughter of James and Emma Loewe. Her father was born in Brighton in 1852, a son of Louis Loewe, a scholar and orientalist of some note. He was sent to France and Germany to learn the languages, became an excellent linguist and was at one time secretary of the Jewish Colonial Trust. Her mother was the daughter of Emanuel Immerwahr, a cornfactor and miller from Upper Silesia; it was from her that Bunny got her love of plants and her skill in making them grow.

After a few years at a dame school in Paddington she went to the Maida Vale High School, where she was not distinguished in her work. She enjoyed games without excelling in them but was not good at lessons, not because she was lazy but because it was her nature to be practical and do things rather than be theoretical and think things out. She would accept lessons when they could be seen to serve her immediate purpose. In a passage in her 'Fifty Years in Stepney' (a series of five talks broadcast on the BBC) she tells us how she managed:

> I remember how I, who could not do ballet dancing, determined after seeing Pavlova that my Girls' Club must do ballet. I discovered Espinoza's magazine with an easy ballet lesson in every issue. I memorised these in bed, practised them whilst dressing the next morning and taught the result to the girls in the evening. Shortly afterwards many dancers, musicians and other artists had been invited to attend a meeting at County Hall where I had to make an impassioned speech, begging them to come to our aid by sending students to help us in clubs. To illustrate our plight I recounted my method of teaching ballet. A note was sent up to me: 'I am so intrigued, do see me afterwards—Adeline Genée'. She came to see me and said 'Go on with your crazy method and I will send a dancer to help you'. She kept her word and two of her company came once a fortnight and took a class. Needless to say I went into the class.

She left school when she was about sixteen and had a year's domestication at home which she quite liked because it was practical. Then came a 'finishing' period with her aunts in Germany where she learnt enough of the language to enjoy reading Thomas Mann and enough music to be enchanted by *Die Meistersinger* and become a Wagnerite, as O.St.G. was to discover.

On her return she worked more seriously at the piano and did a little teaching and accompanying.

Her elder brother, he whom Basil had brought to Oxford, used occasionally to visit Basil at the Club and one evening in 1915 he took Bunny with him. By way of war-work she had taken a training in first aid and joined a Voluntary Aid Detachment; it was arranged that she should take a class in first aid in the O.St.G. club.

When some six months later she had formed the Girls' Club Basil got a report on it from Miss Lily Montagu, who had founded her own girls' club and led it for more than twenty years. 'Miss Loewe', she wrote to him, 'is obviously the right leader. She is bright and full of kindness. One of the girls said to me "When Miss Loewe dances all our club seems to dance". As years go by she will have to make changes of method. I feel she ought to write down the histories of individuals. She thinks it ought not to be necessary.'

The report goes on to say, 'The atmosphere at the end was just what I expected and *you* have created it.' Basil sent it on to Bunny without a covering letter but in the margin opposite the word '*you*' is a gloss in Basil's handwriting which runs 'How? Don't say "indirectly", you know its you.'

The Girls' Club grew and prospered. Lily Caminer drawing on forty years of club membership writes:

There were the camps she started in spite of many difficulties such as insufficient water and a plague of flies, but she overcame them somehow. It was good to discover that 'The Missus' was afraid of thunderstorms and that she burrowed into her pillow. At least there was one chink in her armour.

She helped many people to solve their problems (not always successfully where love was concerned), helped them to develop their talents, helped them with domestic and work troubles and in a thousand other ways.

Sometimes she was a strict disciplinarian but if you were not well she was the most sympathetic and helpful person. Many a member would pop into the club to have a boil cleansed or a wound dressed.

And she was clever at dressmaking and sewing. Although some of the things she made would do credit to an antique dealer's museum, others were lovely and beautifully made. (L.C.)

When she began to have a hand in the Settlement's affairs she let it appear that she had a religion of her own, as Basil well knew. It was a mixture of atavism and simple piety. Her father was staunchly traditional (he had been one of the founders of the North London Synagogue), a good amateur Hebraist and profoundly interested in his religion. Her mother knew the broad outlines of her religion, perhaps with an open mind about reform (her parents had heard Geiger, the great reformist, preaching in Breslau), but she willingly accepted her husband's teaching and arranged her household accordingly. She had a simple God-fearing piety, which she transmitted to her daughter who had not worked at her Hebrew, had little interest in the Law whether Written or Oral but liked such parts of the prayer book and the psalter as went directly to the heart. Of course she joined happily in the singing in the synagogue and in prayers at home. When therefore Basil unfolded to her his 'Judaism without codes' she could respond and make her contribution to it with complete sincerity if with little knowledge. Yet she loved her father and the courage with which he faced the grim problems of one who has to earn his living while steadfastly refusing to work on the Sabbath, and if she continued to the end to keep some of the dietary laws she did it—to use a lapidary expression—in loving memory of her parents.

The Club was nearly twenty years old when Charles Dreyfus first met her.

> She was the queen of the second floor which housed the girls' clubs, a part of the building where mere males feared to tread; occasionally she would appear on the third floor (where I would be sitting in the boys' club) and make some fearsome complaint. A decade later I grew to know her much better through serving on a committee with her and above all through her old standing friendship with my wife[1] whom I had courted from the Settlement. We would regularly visit the Henriques flat after club in the evening and our daughter later adopted her as her god-mother under the name of Auntie Bundles.
>
> She was a women of great fertility of invention, adapting what was available to what was needed; what was available

was likely to be snapped up in unnecessarily large quantities, reducing the cost per unit but sometimes building up surplus stocks. Generous to a fault of her time and her goods she—as well as Basil—was an inveterate hoarder of documents and of anything that might be useful in the future. She had an uncanny knack of making any living room look like a mess, eminently habitable but still a mess. Her fingers were incredibly green so that the chaos of the flat in Berner Street was aggravated by the creepers and flowers in pots everywhere; but if the plants in the flat were helped by vita-glass the flowers in the roof garden which survived or even flourished in the smog of pre-smokeless Stepney owed their condition to her wizardry alone.

Her music-making, religious and secular, permeated the Settlement.

With typically uncalculating boldness she tried to produce the whole of *Die Meistersinger* using Boys' Club voices for the men's parts, but the strain of so many rehearsals was too great and after much heartbreak it had to be scaled down to a performance of some of the scenes, a most creditable achievement which everybody enjoyed. Then she produced Humperdinck's *Hänsel and Gretel*, trebling the Hänsels and Gretels to make up for the thinness of untrained children's voices.

In the Synagogue she was always the choir mistress and 'of course' (her words at the time) she played the organ; that was a family affair, whereas the memorial service at the West London Synagogue was formal and governed by protocol, a word which with its hint of court functionaries mesmerised both Basil and Bunny.

The choir consisted entirely of Club members. Bunny taught them to read tonic sol-fa (which she had first to teach herself) and from that beginning they went on to achieve and maintain a high standard of performance which was universally acclaimed, and did a great deal to attract the local population to the synagogue.

She made choral arrangements of classical music for the services while drawing freely on the traditional hymns and chants. Her ability to transpose freely was invaluable when a singer wobbled off the right key. It was a girls' choir and it

rejoiced her to have in it children and grandchildren of the
original choristers.

As an artist she was exuberant and prolific. She had had
nothing more than the routine school drawing lessons.
Report has it that she took some lessons while she was at
the Settlement, just enough to enable her to use a latent
inherited talent. She respected the professional advice of
my wife, though I doubt if she always followed it. She
became a trustee of the Whitechapel Art Gallery which
staged her one-man show of Vanishing Stepney; it was a
remarkable achievement for a part-time amateur to supply
enough canvases of interest to cover the walls of the
Gallery. Besides the East End, Club and camp life and
scenes from her travels were her usual subjects. Someone
who has a few of her pictures on his walls said, 'All her
pictures have the faults of the untaught, many of them are
of little interest, some of them show a sensitivity to colour
and form and a perception of the essential which makes
me like to look at them.' Some critics called them good
'reportage'. (C.D.)

At the outbreak of war in 1939 she immediately enrolled
in the ARP and was asked to form and command a local
ambulance station. A.G.L., who helped to man the station,
writes:

This was something after her own heart, the donning of
uniform, the inspection and parades, the 'exercises' she
invented, the turn-outs, stop-watch in hand in response to
a mock alert, were all her cup of tea and she ran the place
with such gusto that in a competition the station was
awarded the London trophy (a silver casket) for efficiency.
But that was before the raids began. By the time the
bombs started to fall she had quarrelled with some
high-ranking superior and resigned in a huff. Nothing
daunted she then organised a soup kitchen at the
Settlement and with a small devoted team of club
members went out night after night among the bomb
victims with her mobile canteen.

When the war ended in 1945 she became chairman of

the Germany section of the Jewish Committee for Relief
Abroad and trained with that body to be ready to go to
the help of surviving Jews on the Continent. With the
co-operation of the UNRRA (United Nations
Rehabilitation and Relief Association) and the Army
authorities teams went out to do relief work and she went
with one of them as leader. With her headquarters in Celle
she organised a camp for Jewish refugees in the old SS
barracks of Belsen; the camp itself had been burnt before
she arrived.

There was plenty to do. Hospitals had to be organised,
nurses found and a legal department had to be set up to
deal with problems of nationality, matrimonial status (so
many families had been torn apart) and later on of claims.

Such were the tasks of the teams. Bunny went happily
to work at all of them, making up for inexperience by
inventiveness and temerity. (A.G.L.)

When she came back from Germany she applied herself to
helping under-privileged Jews throughout the world, including
those as remote as the Falashas, the black Jews of Ethiopia. She
became Chairman of the British branch of OSE (Organisatio
Sanitaria Ebraica) which maintained child welfare and general
medical centres in North Africa and the East, and
Vice-Chairman of the British Branch of ORT (Organisation for
Rehabilitation and Training) in which capacities she visited
some of the North African ghettoes to find out the priorities of
their needs. She made her report and when funds had to be
raised to implement it came forward and appealed to the
Jewish public. She had by that time developed her faculty of
public speaking. As far back as 1917 she had read a paper to the
West London Synagogue Association. A social worker whom
Basil greatly trusted wrote to him, 'The paper was delightfully
written, it had real literary merit and a distinct personal charm
by which one was carried away . . . it was daring in conception
and full of a certain freedom of expression . . . its defects were
that vexed questions were either ignored or begged.' Her
speeches were never very profound or intellectual, but they
were sincere, knowledgeable, and expressed with feeling and
freshness; for their purpose they were just right.

One of the administrators of ORT who had worked with her for many years said, 'She may have been difficult in committee but as a propagandist she was splendid.'

Together with all her duties, interests and hobbies in Club, Settlement and Synagogue it makes a long and varied catalogue of work done. She was always busy at something and never stopped. At sixty-five she set up Workrooms for the Elderly in Stepney (she was given her CBE for services to the community in East London); at seventy-two she finished a four-year stint as President of the League of Jewish Women; at seventy-seven she broadcast a series of talks on 'Fifty Years in Stepney', no sociological survey but vivid and in a chatty way informative. At eighty she gave the sixth Basil Henriques Memorial Lecture and until she died she toiled away at Basil's biography.

She was [says Charles Dreyfus] a tireless woman and seemed to need no sleep; she always thought that others were so constituted, for her helpers at the girls' camps would sometimes drop off from exhaustion. She was a born leader and found it difficult to accept a subordinate roll. She was very much the boss in her own clubs and it did not matter terribly if she alienated some of her more spirited helpers. What was sad was her inability to keep on close terms with more than a few of her old girls. Their respect and gratitude she retained but very few could give her the almost unquestioning obedience and devotion which they felt she demanded.

Most of their friends thought that the one big joint mistake of Basil and Bunny was their decision to continue to live in the Settlement after they had retired as wardens; all would have lived more happily had the monarchs who had abdicated voluntarily quitted their royal palace. Yet they remained and tended to become mute reproaches when changes were made. The reason was that their hearts were in the East End. Bunny fought to the end of her life to maintain the Settlement's activities there, though its trustees knew that the clientèle had moved elsewhere. Yet in her closing years she actively helped in the setting up of its new clubs in North London, composing fresh songs for its inauguration.

Rose Henriques was one of the most remarkable, difficult,

capable, gifted, infuriating and generous women of her time. We were proud to count her among our friends. (C.D.)

Bunny and Basil had enough in common to form the basis of a marriage of minds or a partnership in sublimation. Neither was much given to strict logical thought, she far less than he; like some dictators they sometimes thought with their blood. Neither was by nature a student or a theorist but both were at their best when there was a call for devotion to a cause, energy and that strange ambivalent form of self-assertiveness called 'leadership'. Each had inherited a tradition in which the claims of religion to be the basis of moral conduct were unchallenged and each had found that the religious framework of their youth did not satisfy them in their maturity. Finally each liked to have his own way and to rule his own roost. Such qualities make for close co-operation punctuated by intermittent storms.

Storms or no [writes A.G.L.] Basil knew and always readily acknowledged that without Bunny he could not have made the Settlement into the vital busy inspiring centre that it became. It was her remarkable gifts of imaginative resourcefulness and inventiveness which together with his qualities caught and held the enthusiasm and devotion of young and old.

Notes

1 Childhood

1 I am indebted to Dr A. S. Diamond for the facts on which this comment is based.
2 From *The Indiscretions of a Warden*, Methuen, 1937, p. 13.

2 Harrow and Oxford

1 Scholar, theologian and philanthropist. He had been at Balliol under Jowett and was Hibbert lecturer in 1892; his publications are regarded as among the most important in Bible studies.
2 Oxford House (1884) was founded in Bethnal Green by the Oxford Pastorate in the same year as Toynbee Hall in Whitechapel. Its purpose was to supply a headquarters where university men could learn about the real condition of the artisan and labouring classes in East London, to study their problems on the spot and to take part in the furtherance of Christianity and education and the bettering of moral and hygienic conditions. Toynbee Hall, where Basil was to go when he left Oxford, had similar purposes but was intended by its founder, Canon S. Barnett, to be undenominational.
3 The Oxford Medical Mission was the settlement founded in Bermondsey in 1897 by Oxford Evangelicals and built up by John Stansfeld who created its Christian tradition of self-sacrificing work. From it sprang the group of boys' clubs known as the Oxford and Bermondsey Clubs. It is often referred to as the Oxford and Bermondsey Mission.
4 Basil was fond of his two aunts, Alice and Beatrice, and continued to visit them as much for his pleasure as for theirs, perhaps because they were linked with his past.
5 Loewe returned to Cambridge in 1931 to be Reader in Rabbinics.

3   Apprenticeship

1   See thereon W. J. Fishman, *East End Radicals*.
2   Chevra. Literally 'brotherhood'. It also denotes a conventicle which serves a group as a place for prayer and religious study.
3   Toynbee Hall. See Chapter 2, note 2.
4   The Charity Organisation Society was founded in 1869; it sought to co-ordinate charitable effort and in any given case to ascertain the appropriate remedy by investigation. In 1944 it became the Family Welfare Organisation.
5   Robin Montefiore was C.G.M.'s son Leonard, known to his friends as Robin.
6   Lady Bullock and Evelyn were the wife and daughter of Sir George Bullock, Governor of Bermuda whom Basil had met when he visited his brother Ronald (see p. 17, above). He may be referring to the then Duchess of Sutherland who took an active interest in social problems.
7   Probably H. K. Stein whom Basil had known at Oxford; as a manager of the Club he saw it through some of its early difficulties.
8   'Common' because the lodgers occupy one common room for the purpose of eating and sleeping. They have been controlled and regulated by the Public Health Acts under which the keepers must be registered. See now the Health Services and Public Health Act 1968. They were defined in the Public Health Act 1936, S. 235.

4   Birth of a Club

1   The first word of a passage from the Pentateuch (Deut. VI: 4‑9) in Hebrew containing creedal statements of the unity of God and the duty to love Him and to teach that duty to one's children; perhaps as well known to Jews as Matthew VI: 9-13 is to Christians.
2   The best known edition in Great Britain of the Jewish Daily Prayer Book, with an unsurpassed English translation.
3   This was Mr H. Dombey who joined the Club in 1916 and became a close friend and confidant of Basil and Bunny.
    He spent most of his spare time in the administration and day-to-day work of the clubs, one of which he founded and managed. He was a founder-member of the synagogue of which he is still (1976) a vice-president, and both he and his wife were on the Executive Committee of the Settlement. For many of the relevant facts I have had recourse to his memories of sixty years' voluntary personal service.

5   Preacher into Soldier

1   The name of the magazine edited by Bunny for the Club members in the forces. It began as a small informal budget of news and extracts

from letters.

2 Basil had always called her Bunny and to the Club she was 'the Missus' (just as he was either 'the Long 'un' or 'the Gaffer'); so from now onward she had better be Bunny.

3 This was the embryo of *Prayers for Trench and Base*, which was issued from the Chief Rabbi's Office, together with the Chief Rabbi's *Book of Jewish Thoughts*. A third impression was published in 1940.

4 This was news of the engagement of David Caminer and Lily Kay the sister of Sam Kay; the marriage took place in 1924. David Caminer and Sam Kay were original members of the Club. Caminer, who died in 1975, had been on the Settlement Council and Chairman of its executive committee; he was warden for a year or two after Basil left. In the First World War he was in the Royal Flying Corps. In the Second he was acting wing-commander in the RAF. There was no boy in the Club for whom Basil had a greater respect.

Kay was a lay reader from the earliest days of the Synagogue, was president for many years and still is. It is largely due to him that the congregation still exists. Lily Caminer built up and ran the club for young children—'the 1924 club'—and was a chorister for some forty years.

5 One of the best known war correspondents of his time. He was on the staff of the *Daily Mail*.

6   Warden of a Settlement

1 A wealthy bullion-broker who was one of the original members of the Club and served it continuously as honorary treasurer and firm friend for over fifty years; he lived at the Club and, one might almost say, for it.

2 Such as the industrialist Leon Rees who for some forty years put his great administrative competence at the service of the Settlement; or the five members of the Lynes family who created and for seventeen years managed a panel of fund-raisers and brought in many thousands of pounds.

3 The givers were Viscount Bearsted and his son Walter (the father and brother of that Gerald Samuel—killed in the war—whose club Basil had admired so much during his apprentice years) together with the congregation of the West London Synagogue.

4 Col. Sir Frederic Stern.

5 Mr Leonard Montefiore had lent it to the Central British Fund for a sanatorium and later gave it to the trustees of the Settlement.

6 Basil gave these figures to a conference of social workers in 1919.

7 In 1934 he won the light-weight championship in the Amateur Boxing Association contest.

8 A 'General Relief Fund' had been created in aid of Spanish women and children in distress caused by the civil war; some of the children had been offered asylum in the United Kingdom.

9   So called after the Cambridge graduate who was killed in the First World War; see p.20, above.

10 A certain amplitude in this respect may reflect Basil's friendship with the directors of one of the leading catering firms.

11 Cupboard or recess which contains the sepharim or scrolls of parchment manuscripts of the Pentateuch.

12 In the letter he says, 'I had heard so much about you and your work from my father and mother.'

13 Literally 'teaching' but generally applied to the Pentateuch.

14 I am indebted to Mr Alfred Diamond, OBE, JP, for information from which the following abstract is taken:

The Bernhard Baron Settlement in Henriques Street was closed in September 1973.

The following are the affiliates of the Bernhard Baron Settlement.

The Oxford and St George's (West London) Jewish Clubs and Centre, Ealing.

The Oxford and St George's (North London) Jewish Clubs and Community Centre, Barnet.

The Synagogue and the Old Boys and Old Girls Clubs meet in the Stepney Jewish Settlement, Tower Hamlets.

The Friendship Club meets at the Brady Club in Hanbury Street, E.1.

7   Magistrate

1   Probably the General Strike of 1926.

2   He was lucky too in his panel. Among them were Phyllis Gerson, MBE, who subsequently became chairman and was herself warden of a settlement; Miriam Moses, OBE, a woman of great character born and bred in the East End, also warden of a settlement and a club; Lady Cynthia Colville, DCVO, DBE, an experienced social worker who often took the chair; the Hon. Mrs W. McGowan, who later became a vice-president of the NABC; and Mrs Michael Stewart whose husband was later to become Foreign Secretary under the Labour government.

3   From *The Courage of his Convictions* by Tony Parker and Robert Allerton, with acknowledgments to Hutchinson & Co.

4   I thank the Association for their help with this topic.

8   The Day's Work

1   All boy offenders were sent to Wandsworth, either on remand or to await disposal.

2   A place of residence for persons of unsound mind, then known as a lunatic asylum.

3   The idea of a national association may have been conceived in the mind of W. McG. Eagar, author of *Making Men*, when he was in France in the First World War; he was one of the founders of the NABC.

4   In their Annual Report for 1961–2.

5   The Local Government Act, 1929, had removed from them the stigma of being under the Destitution Authority.

6   The Hon. Sir Sidney Holland, who became the 2nd Viscount Knutsford, was chairman from 1896 to 1931; these extracts from his correspondence with Basil show something of the spirit in which he worked for the hospital.

   The London Hospital very kindly read part of this section and furnished me with some of the facts.

7   Lord Knutsford was known as the 'Prince of Beggars' through his fund-raising work for hospitals.

8   In *Indiscretions of a Warden*.

9   He had ceased to be President of the Board of Education but was still an MP.

10 He had introduced them in his Education Act of 1918 but they were caught by the economy measures of 1920—the Geddes Axe—and did not come into operation.

9   1939 to 1945. The Settlement Carries On

1   See Chapter 5, note 1.

2   Mr A. J. Diamond, OBE, JP, a member of the Club who became a very active member of the executive committee of the Settlement and Bernard Prins who had been for some time Basil's sub-warden.

3   Commemorating the re-dedication of the second Temple by the Maccabaean Resistance ca. 165 BC.

4   From the *Anniversary Review*. Permission to quote from it was given by the Old Boy who anonymously defrayed the cost of its production.

5   When war broke out in 1914 J. B. Brunel Cohen was on the Reserve of Officers in the Territorial Army. He was mentioned in despatches and although he lost both legs he managed until his death in 1965 to lead an active life of public service mainly on behalf of the wounded and disabled, and was an MP for thirteen years. He gave much time to the British Legion of which he was honorary treasurer and vice-chairman. He was knighted in 1943 and made a KBE in 1948.

6   From the *Anniversary Review*.

7   Then Parliamentary Secretary to the Ministry of Home Security.

8   For an account of this tour see pp.123–6.

9   A commodious cottage near Leighton Buzzard put at their disposal by Mrs Leopold de Rothschild whose house at Ascott was nearby.

10 A secondary school to which promising pupils from other schools in the neighbourhood might be sent.

11 From the *Manchester Guardian*.

10   On the Warpath, or
the Technique of Making a Fuss

1 Cmd 2561, presented in 1926.
2 E.g. the Association for Moral and Spiritual Hygiene, the Joint Committee of Voluntary Societies on Sexual Offences, the National Council of Women, the Committee on Psychiatry and the Law appointed jointly by the British Medical Association and the Magistrates' Association.
3 Cmd 1191 of 1960.
4 They said that they could not support 'the precise recommendations' made by Basil but had the greatest sympathy with his objectives.
5 Now the Crown Court.
6 Lord Kilmuir, formerly Sir David Fyfe, QC.
7 In fact the Court had that power but Basil wanted it extended to include other than sexual cases.
8 These points had been considered by the Ingleby Committee and recommendations along these lines had been made.
9 A copy of the letter was made available to H.R.H. the Duke of Edinburgh.
10 Lord of Appeal in Ordinary.
11 Master of the Rolls.
12 Formerly Sir Norman Birkett, Lord Justice of Appeal.
13 Wife of the Master of Trinity and a member of the Ingleby Committee.
14 What 'the lawyers' feared was the risk of depriving an accused person of the right to cross-examine his accuser searchingly.
15 The Rt Hon. Jo Grimond, PC, MP, then leader of the Liberal Party.
16 The Rt Hon. J. Chuter Ede, CH, JP, DL, MP, had been Home Secretary 1945-51.
17 Mr Jeremy Thorpe, MP, subsequently leader of the Liberal Party.
18 Member of the Home Office Advisory Council on the Treatment of Offenders.
19 He wrote to the National Association for Mental Health, the National Society for the Prevention of Cruelty to Children, the Church of England Childrens' Council, the Norwood Jewish Orphanage, the Jewish Welfare Board, the London Diocesan Council for Moral Welfare, the Church of England Moral Welfare Council, the National Federation of Parent Teachers Associations, the National Association of Mixed Clubs and Girls' Clubs, the National Union of Teachers, the National Union of Women Teachers, two local branches of the Townswomen's Guild, the British Medical Association, the British Paediatric Association, the Institute of Psychiatry, the Howard League for Penal Reform and the London Police Court Mission.
20 Children and Young Persons Act, 1963, S. 28.
21 Ibid., S. 27.
22 Ibid., S. 57.

23 These facts are strangley in contrast with Dr Weizmann's assertion in 'Trial and Error', p.536, that his opponents were a few rich and powerful people who did not know much about it.

24 The office in St Swithin's Lane of the firm of N. M. Rothschild & Sons as it then was.

25 Among those whom he consulted were Rabbi H. Marmorstein, PhD, Mr R.J. Loewe, MC, MA, and the Rev. I. Slotki, MBE, Litt D.

26 The Board of Deputies was the 'London Committee of Deputies of British Jews' founded in 1760. It is primarily concerned with the political and civil rights of British Jewry. The Anglo-Jewish Association was founded in 1871 to promote the cultural and social welfare of Jews. According to the *Jewish Year Book*, membership is open to 'all British Jews who accept as their guiding principle loyalty to their faith and their country'.

27 Col. Sir Louis Gluckstein, GBE, TD, QC, DL as he now is.

12   Basil's Religion

1 So it was put to me by Rabbi Hugo Gryn, of the West London Synagogue of British Jews, who regarded Basil's life as an expression of the aims and purposes of the congregation in which he had been brought up.

2 H. M. Adler, editor of *The Service of the Synagogue*, published by Routledge, 1906; see ibid., 'Service of the New Year', p.242.

3 From *Outlines of Liberal Judaism* ch. XIX, p.302.

4 Miss S. Prins, at one time a teacher under the LCC, built up a very successful play centre. In *Indiscretions of a Warden*, p.89, Basil calls her 'our devoted friend and right-hand man'.

5 Rabbi Kopul Rosen, founder and first headmaster of Carmel College.

6 See his article in the *Jewish Chronicle*, 1961.

7 A 'Talmud Torah', literally 'study of the Pentateuchal Law and teachings', is a school maintained by a community for the teaching of Hebrew and religious knowledge.
    A 'Cheder', literally 'room', is a small private school or class for the same purpose.

13   Turning Point

1 He was succeeded by two very competent professionally trained social workers, Myer and Miriam Sopel.

15   Retrospect

1 *Remembering my Good Friends* by Mary Hamilton, p.97, cited in *East End Radicals* by W. J. Fishman.

2 From a paper on 'The Sociological Background of the Soldier'.
3 Sir Reginald Goodwin, CBE, for many years General Secretary of the NABC.

16   R.L.H.

1 Enid Abrahams, who married Charles Dreyfus in 1947, was an artist by profession as well as an altruist by nature. She served the Settlement as a voluntary worker for over thirty years, looking after the activities of art, drama and debate, and supporting Bunny with staunch friendship and discreet advice until her lamented death in 1972.